I0711177

BORDERLINE PERSONALITY DISORDER

HOW TO STOP ANXIETY AND DEPRESSION WALKING WITH THE SKILLS OF DIALECTICAL BEHAVIORAL THERAPY. HOW TO PREVENT OUT-OF-CONTROL EMOTIONS FROM DESTROYING YOUR RELATIONSHIPS LIKE EGGSHELLS

Table of Contents

Introduction

The thoughts that surround personality disorders has gained a lot of stigma in recent years. Many people are scared by what they will have seen on television or in books and they will often see the person with the disorder not as someone they should associate with, but as someone who is to be feared because they are off or going to do something that is crazy. This guidebook is going to take a look into one of these personality disorders, borderline personality disorder, and help you to discover what it is, if you or a loved one has it, and that it is not the person who is strange and wrong, but the disorder that is preventing that person from living the life that they would like.

tarts out with an excellent summary on what this kind of personality disorder is about. It will take some time to look at a brief description of the signs and symptoms, some of the available treatment options, and even how others will be able to help.

When goes into the meat of the issue a bit more and talks about some of the causes that can start borderline personality disorder. This chapter talks about how it is not entirely understood what causes this kind of disorder and how some facts can be present in those who do not have the disorder. Some of the factors that might be present in those with this disorder, especially if they are mixed together include genetics, brain abnormalities, neurobiological factors, developmental factors, as well as some other things.

One of the best ways that you are going to be able to determine if you or someone else has this kind of disorder is to look for some of the signs and symptoms. There are a lot of different symptoms that can be found with this disorder and this chapter is going to split them up into different categories to make it easier to see where each of them lie. Some of the different signs and symptoms that you will be able to see in a person who has this kind of disorder include emotional symptoms, behavior symptoms, self-harm, interpersonal relationship issues, issues with their own sense of self, and cognition problems.

Talks a bit about how this kind of disorder is going to be diagnosed and some of the ways that you will be able to get a diagnosis from the therapist. Some of the topics that will be discussed in this chapter include the subtypes of the disorder, when the disorder will show up, how to diagnose it when other disorders are present, and so on. One of the best things that a person with this disorder is going to be able to do for themselves is to get a diagnosis so that they can get the kind of treatment that they need. Unfortunately, this kind of help is not always available to patients because they are not diagnosed or they are not willing to get the help that is needed.

Talks about what is going to happen once a diagnosis is made and the client has agreed to get the help that they need. This chapter talks about the management and prognosis that will occur during this phase. For the most part, therapy is the best option and this is what is going to be recommended for most patients. There are some cases where the person is going to need some medications to help out though. These are not going to be used in place of the therapy thought; they are often used to treat a few of the symptoms of the disorder or to help out if there are some other issues that are at play and can make the treatment much more effective.

Next is and it is going to talk a bit about the steps that are going to need to be taken to properly deal with this kind of personality disorder. It is going to start out with some of the steps that the family will be able to do to help out their loved one with their personality disorder to help out with the treatment. It will then go into some more details about what a person who has the disorder is able to do to give themselves the best chance at recovery. Recovery is possible for those who have this disorder, but they need to be willing to work for it and keep working and trusting the therapist to see the best results.

Finally, s going to take a look at some of the controversies that come with this kind of disorder. There are many people who think that those with this disorder are big liars and that they either do not have the disorder or if they do, they are just going to lie about it to the therapist and will never be able to get healed the way that they should. This chapter will go on to talk about some of the stigma that can come with borderline personality disorder, and how society and culture has been portrayed to the mass population.

As you can see, there is a lot of information about this kind of disorder and it can be confusing. It does not help matters that some of the symptoms of this disorder are going to be similar to some of the other disorders that are out there so it is hard to recognize and diagnose the disorder in some people. Use this guidebook to start getting a better understanding of the disorder and to help those who may be going through the issue right now in their lives and simply need the right treatment and support to make things better.

Chapter 1 The World of the Borderline Disorder

Also known as talk therapy, psychotherapy is a treatment approach that involves a variety of types, such as dialectical behavior therapy, cognitive behavioral therapy, mentalization-based therapy, schema-focused therapy, and transference-focused psychotherapy.

Like with any other personality disorder, psychotherapy is commonly used to treat patients to help them overcome their problem. It is important to take note that even though medications can be effective solutions for symptoms, they may have unpleasant side effects.

In addition, medications cannot help patients learn emotion regulation, coping skills, and other important skills that they can use to improve their life. In addition, a major objective of psychotherapy is to prevent a person with a personality disorder from committing suicide.

It is crucial to assess and monitor the tendency to become suicidal all throughout the whole course of treatment. When a person with borderline personality disorder displays severe symptoms, they may need to receive medication or even undergo hospitalization.

The following types of psychotherapy should be tried first, before choosing a more invasive treatment procedure.

Cognitive Behavioral Therapy

Cognitive behavioral therapy involves working with a mental health counselor to become more aware of negative, ineffective, and inaccurate thinking. Patients also work with a therapist so they can see challenging situations more objectively and clearly. In addition, they work with a therapist so they can learn how to practice alternative solution techniques.

What can you expect from it? Well, cognitive behavior therapy focuses mainly on the present moment. This means that you should not dwell on your past experiences. You are still allowed to explain how you came to behave or think the way you do, but you should focus on how you think and act at the present.

Cognitive behavior therapy is also directive. You can expect the therapist to be active during every session. He/she will give you direct advice. In other therapies, the therapists mostly sit back and listen while the patients direct the session.

In addition, in cognitive behavioral therapy, the therapists generally assume that your symptoms are associated with the behavior and thinking patterns that you have adapted throughout the years. Hence, they do not believe that simply spending one to two hours per week in therapy is enough to produce significant results.

They are most likely to give homework and let the patients work on changing their behavior and thinking patterns outside of therapy sessions. Before a session ends, homework sheets and handouts are usually given.

Dialectical Behavior Therapy

Dialectical behavior therapy is especially designed to treat borderline personality disorder. In general, it is done through phone counseling, individual sessions, and group sessions. It makes use of a skills-based approach combined with meditation and physical exercises to help patients learn how to regulate their emotions, improve relationships, and tolerate distress.

During individual therapy, the individual therapist is the main therapist and the patient undergoes individual therapy sessions. The patient goes to the office of the therapist to talk about their thoughts and feelings among other things.

During telephone contact, the patient speaks to the therapist via telephone in between therapy sessions. However, it is important to note that telephone contact is not done for the purpose of psychotherapy. Instead, it provides the patient the support and help that they need to apply the skills that they have learned to real life situations, as well as to help them avoid injuring themselves.

The patient may also call their therapist if they want to mend any issues between them prior to the next therapy session. However, they're not allowed to call within the next twenty-four hours if they injure themselves. This is to avoid the reinforcement of self-injury.

In skills training, a patient speaks with a therapist along with a group of people with the same condition. These patients are taught skills that may be useful to their daily situations. These skills include core mindfulness skills, emotion modulation skills, interpersonal effectiveness skills, and distress tolerance skills.

Core mindfulness skills are based on certain Buddhist meditation techniques, but without any religious allegiance involved. Such techniques are used to enable the patients to be more aware of their experiences, as well as to develop the ability to be mindful of the present moment.

Interpersonal effectiveness skills focus on achieving one's goals with other people. The patients are taught how to ask for what they want, refuse requests or offers, maintain good relationships with other people, and improve their self-esteem.

Emotion modulation skills are about ways to change distressing emotional states. Distress tolerance skills, on the other hand, include techniques for dealing with such emotional states if it is not possible for them to be changed.

In therapist consultation groups, the therapists receive dialectical behavior therapy from one another. The members of the group have to stay focused. They are also required to give a formal undertaking to stay in dialectical behavior therapy mode and avoid making pejorative remarks against the other members.

Schema-Focused Therapy

Schema-focused therapy combines different approaches of therapies, particularly emotion-based techniques and cognitive behavior therapy, to help patients evaluate repetitive life themes and life patterns so they can identify positive patterns and correct negative ones. It focuses on helping them change negative and long-standing self-images through letter writing, role-playing, anger management, assertiveness training, relaxation, guided imagery, and gradual exposure to situations that induce anxiety.

Limited re-parenting is one unique key element of schema-focused therapy. Here, the patients are able to establish a secure attachment to their therapist. This is, of course, within the bounds of a professional relationship. According to Dr. Joan Farrell, director of the Schema Therapy Institute Midwest Indianapolis Center, many people with borderline personality disorder missed emotional learning when they were younger. They were not encouraged to express their needs and emotions.

They also did not receive adequate validation, which is why their core childhood needs are met in schema therapy. Their therapist ensures that such needs are met by expressing compassion, providing nurturance, and setting limitations. After the therapy, patients are expected to become healthy emotionally. They are also expected to be autonomous enough so they will no longer need their therapist to meet their core needs. Instead, they should be able to meet such needs on their own.

Mentalization-Based Therapy

Mentalization-based therapy is a type of psychodynamically-oriented psychotherapy that helps patients identify and isolate their feelings and thoughts from those of other people. It mainly focuses on thinking before reacting. Patients who undergo this treatment are taught how to separate their feelings and thoughts from the feelings and thoughts of other people.

Individuals with borderline personality disorder usually have intense and unstable relationships that cause them to manipulate or exploit other people unconsciously. They are not able to recognize the effects of their behavior on other people. Through, mentalization, they can learn how to understand feelings and behavior, as well as associate these elements with specific mental states.

According to research, individuals with borderline personality disorder do not have a high capacity for mentalization. You should take note that mentalization is a crucial component in traditional psychotherapy. In mentalization-based therapy, its concept is emphasized, practiced and reinforced within a supportive and safe psychotherapy setting. Mentalization-based therapy is less directive than cognitive behavior therapy.

Transference-Focused Psychotherapy

Transference-focused psychotherapy is also commonly referred to as psychodynamic psychotherapy. It aims to help patients understand their interpersonal and emotional difficulties through the development of relationships between them and their therapists. One of its most distinguishable features is its emphasis on the psychological structure that underlies the symptoms of borderline personality disorder.

Transference-focused psychotherapy also focuses on a deep psychological setup in which the mind is structured around a fundamental split that identifies a way of experiencing oneself and ones surroundings. Such a split determines the perceptions of the patient and results in impulsive self-destructive behaviors and chaotic interpersonal relations. It was actually based on a model of the mind wherein early affectively charged experiences have been established in the psychological structure of the patient.

When you undergo this treatment, you will be taught how to apply your insights into real situations. Your beliefs, attitudes, and internal images will be transferred onto your therapist. By examining this transference, you will be able to work through the distorted images that you automatically impose on external reality. Over time, your capacity for self-reflection will increase and you will be able to adapt to life better. Conversely, your symptoms of borderline personality disorder will decrease.

Every patient needs to be in a structured therapeutic setting, no matter what type of therapy he or she goes through. Individuals with borderline personality disorder usually try to test the limitations of their therapist during treatment. Hence, it is important to establish a well-defined and proper boundary at the beginning of the therapy session.

Clinicians should be aware of their feelings towards their patients, especially when the latter start to show inappropriate behaviors. People with this type of personality disorder tend to be discriminated against unfairly because others see them as troublemakers. A lot of people do not understand the true nature of their condition, which is why they are often shunned.

Dr. Phillip Long notes that these patients may actually need more care than other patients and that their rowdy behavior may only be caused by their personality disorder. He also notes that a therapeutic alliance must develop within the treatment and experiences of the patient with their therapist.

Moreover, the therapists should be tolerant despite repeated episodes of rage, fear, and distrust of their patients. They should also avoid uncovering to boost ego defenses, so the patients can be less anxious about loss and fragmentation. The main goals of therapy must not be in terms of complete personality restructuring, but rather in terms of life gains towards independent functioning.

That is Borderline Personality Disorder?

Have you ever met a person you hated on sight? Someone who appears callous, selfish, and reckless, without a care for consequences? You don't say anything, but you secretly loathe this person who seems to get on everybody's nerves. Or do you have a friend who has a hard time keeping her emotions in check, who doesn't seem to have a lot of friends because of her aggressive and combative tendencies? How about that promiscuous girl who seems to enjoy displaying risqué behavior in public?

Don't be so quick to judge. You may not be aware of it, but this person is probably suffering from something known as Borderline Personality Disorder (BPD). It may sound weird or foreign to the ears, but people with BPD tend to exhibit impulsivity and a tendency to engage in dangerous activities. They can also be aggressive and quarrelsome against people who stand in their way. Often capricious, impulsive, and reckless, these people have few friends and lasting relationships.

Definition

The term BPD caused much confusion for many people who aren't familiar with this personality disorder and its symptoms, which is why the World Health Organization gave it a new name, Emotionally Unstable Personality Disorder. It was first diagnosed in 1980.

People who suffer from BPD tend to be impulsive, capricious and reckless, going after what they want without giving a damn to the consequences. They are also prone to emotional, explosive outbursts, and could turn nasty to people who oppose their actions.

In the long run, people with BPD exhibit a persistent pattern of being unable to maintain close interpersonal relationships. They also tend to have a disturbance in their self-image and the way they feel and express emotions.

BPD usually develops during the early adult years (late teens to early 20s). The impulsivity and instability of relationships may have already been present in recent years, usually driven by the individual's self-image and social experiences. They might even appear shallow and capricious to most other people.

BPD is said to affect two percent of the global population, with female patients more than males. About 7 out of 10 cases of reported and diagnosed BPD are female. BPD may reach its peak during the first few years after its onset, but with proper therapy and treatment, it usually lessens in intensity as the subject grows old. Most patients outgrow its most severe symptoms by the time they reach their 40s or 50s.

Symptoms

As a behavioral disorder, most of the symptoms of BPD have something to do with a person's actions, emotions, and tendencies. The following are just some of the most common symptoms and characteristics of someone who has BPD.

Fear of abandonment

Contrary to being emotionally shallow, BPD individuals are actually full of emotional scars and insecurities. They don't have a lot of self-respect, and they often feel that everyone they care about is going to leave them. In response, they take extra effort to make sure that the people they love won't abandon them.

Unstable relationships

For years, a BPD patient might have difficulty holding on to relationships. He might have a conflicted relationship with his family, or might flit from one romantic relationship to the next. This might be due to an idealized view of relationships, and then disillusionment when reality becomes less than what he expected. They might be clingy to relationships at one time, and bored the next moment.

Disturbed self-image

BPD individuals aren't sure about themselves. They are insecure, and their self-image is constantly changing. They might affiliate themselves with a certain group, and then decide that it doesn't define them. They might follow fads, join cliques, but eventually change their minds about them.

Impulsivity

There's nothing that defines BPD more than reckless impulsivity, which often manifests in risky, potentially dangerous behavior. Individuals with BPD may exercise that impulsivity in different ways, such as reckless driving, overspending, unsafe sex, and even substance abuse.

Suicidal tendencies

BPD individuals often use self-harm and threats as a form of self-defense and manipulation. As such, they might have suicidal tendencies or threats to hurt themselves in order to get what they want. Suicidal behavior is said to be present for 80 percent of reported cases of BPD. Self-harming behavior, on the other hand, is often a result of trying to manage emotions, feelings of guilt or self-blame, or as a means of getting attention from the ones they love.

Mood swings

People who have BPD tend to have extreme varying of moods, which might range from depression, anxiety, irritability, or extreme happiness which only last between a few hours to a few days.

Feeling empty

BPD individuals might feel as if there is something wrong with them, usually feeling like something is missing inside. They feel blank and empty, making them desperate for the love and approval of other people.

Anger management issues

Along with impulsivity, a person who has BPD might have difficulties controlling his anger and temper. They may have anger management issues, along with frequent tantrums or getting into fights. These individuals have excessive hostility and negative emotions, which they cannot control most of the time.

Paranoia

Worse cases of BPD might exhibit fleeting symptoms of paranoia, usually related to stress. They might also have dissociative symptoms ("split personality") because of their varying moods and unstable emotions.

Psychosis

In severe cases, individuals with BPD might experience hallucinations and delusions as part of their symptoms. This is why it was originally called "Borderline Personality" because experts originally thought patients were experiencing a borderline form of another psychotic illness.

Extreme reactions

When a person with BPD feels threatened or fears that she is being abandoned, they tend to lash out with extreme responses and reactions, which may range from extreme depression, panic, or even rage.

These symptoms may manifest as a result of even the pettiest events or occurrences in the person's life. A person with BPD may feel panicked (extreme separation anxiety) even when they become separated from the people they care about for a short time period.

Causes

Like other mental disorders, there is little research to support what are the actual causes of BPD. However, experts generally agree that both environmental and genetic factors are at play when it comes to this disorder.

Genetic factors

There is strong evidence that suggests that BPD is most likely a hereditary illness, especially since a child may inherit certain traits and temperament of his parents, including aggression and impulsivity.

Sociocultural factors

A person's environment and community may have a direct effect to developing BPD. Peer pressure, coupled with poor judgment may lead individuals to make foolish and dangerous choices.

Familial relationships

An individual's relation to his family also plays a major role in the onset of BPD. A person who comes from a dysfunctional family may be more at risk to develop BPD than someone who has a "normal" familial background. Domestic violence and child abuse might also be contributing factors.

Trauma, abuse and neglect are all possible factors, and symptoms might already be present during childhood. However, diagnosis of BPD cannot be officially made unless the patient is already 18 years old. Treatment is difficult but possible, although it tends to take years before full recovery can be made.

Subtypes

The WHO recognizes several major subtypes of BPD individuals, categorized according to the most apparent symptoms that they display:

The discouraged type of BPD individual has avoidant tendencies, coupled with a melancholic mood and a tendency to be overdependent on other people. These individuals are mostly submissive and humble, with feelings of being victimized repeatedly. They have a constant feeling of depression, emptiness and hopelessness because they feel they are powerless to do anything on their own.

The petulant type, on the other hand, features mostly pessimistic and negativistic symptoms of BPD. These people are often restless, defiant, and often impatient. They can get sullen and resentful when they don't get what they want. BPD individuals who fall under this category tend to be very sensitive—they are easily offended and disillusioned.

The impulsive type of BPD features mostly antisocial or histrionic tendencies. These individuals might appear flighty and capricious, promiscuous even to some. They are easily distracted, and they tend to become clingy in relationships because they have an inner fear of loss. They become anxious, irritable or depressed at times, and might even resort to suicide in order to get attention.

Self-destructive BPD individuals have masochistic and melancholic features. These individuals may be reclusive and introverted, with a tendency to be moody and depressive. They stop conforming or becoming pliant (traits of the discouraged subtype) and their anger becomes directed to themselves, leading to suicidal tendencies.

Coping mechanisms

The behaviors displayed by people with BPD are often a form of self-defense and a means of coping with their symptoms. BPD individuals often react negatively and extremely because they feel like they are a victim, whether of other people or of certain circumstances. They feel misunderstood, and often maltreated by other people.

These people don't see their behavior as dangerous or risky, and when things go wrong, they blame it readily on other people. They turn irrational and forget to see both the positive and negative aspects of a situation. They are also prone to self-pity, and constantly seek assurance and comfort from other people.

Chapter 2 The Borderline Society

There are a lot of different disorders that a person is able to get in their lifetime. Some may have issues with wanting to have everything be in the proper place while others may not get along with others and so much more. But this book is not going to spend time talking and worrying about those kinds of disorders. Instead, it is going to spend a lot of time going on about the disorder that is known as borderline personality disorder.

Borderline personality disorder is actually a cluster B personality disorder and will be marked with impulsivity, instability, and the person is going to have troubles with their own self-image and interpersonal relationships. Basically, it is a mental illness that is going to cause some intense behaviors in the person who is suffering from them. The people who are undergoing this kind of disorder will find that they have severe problems determining what their self-worth is, engage in impulsive behaviors in the hopes of getting an adrenaline rush and without care to how much it could hurt them and others, and very intense mood swings for no reason. If you know someone who has this disorder, you will notice that all of their relationships are troubled, whether it is with parents, siblings, friends, love interests, or coworkers.

In most of the cases, the signs for this kind of disorder are going to appear during their childhood, but the issues are not going to be present until they get a little bit older and enter early adulthood. The treatments for this kind of condition are going to be hard and it is not going to be something that will be done in just a few days or even weeks; this condition is going to take many years to heal and many times it never happens.

So you may be curious as to what is causing this disorder to occur. Unfortunately, experts are not in agreement at the exact causes of borderline personality disorders. Some believe that there are some issues with the chemicals inside the brain, the ones that control your mood and that these are to blame for some people developing the disorder. It also looks like this disorder is carried through families so if you have someone in your family tree that had the disorder, your risk of developing it may go up.

Often, you will find that this kind of personality disorder is going to appear when the person had a childhood trauma of some kind. This could include a death of a close relative or their parent, being neglected, or being severely abused. The risk becomes higher when the child who is going through this trauma also has issues with coping with the stresses and anxieties that are around them. What this means is that just because a child has had a trauma in their life during childhood does not mean that this trauma is going to make them have borderline personality disorder. It does increase the chances of that occurring, but basically if they have a lot of trouble with fears, dealing with things that are happening around them, and do not like change, it is more likely that they are going to develop the disorder if some trauma does occur in their childhood.

For the most part, those with this kind of disorder are not going to get the help that they need. They are not going to recognize that they have any issues at all and so they are not going to get any help. Also, they have pushed away a lot of their own loved ones to the point that they do not have a lot of people who are going to want to have anything to do with them. This makes it very unlikely that they are going to have someone see that there is a problem and will get them the help that they need. This means that the person with the disorder is probably going to go without treatment unless something else comes up and then they are going to be stuck with this condition for the rest of their lives.

For those who are lucky enough to get treatment, they need to be able and willing to take the treatment that they are given. Many of those with this condition are not able to trust their therapists or do not think that they are going to need to stick around for a long time in order to get it done and so they will not get the proper help and will fail. They are going to need to find a therapist who is willing to stick with them and help out and they will need a lot of support to get through this time and seek the help that they need. If they are able to do this, they are more than likely going to succeed since this is what the statistics have pointed out in the past for other patients.

The symptoms are important to look for so that those around the person can get them the help that they need. Most of the time, the sufferer is not going to be able to see that they have a problem and at times they may not admit that anything is wrong at all.

Signs and Symptoms: A Summary

Sometimes, the issues with this disorder are hard to discover because everyone has times when they are struggling with their behaviors and emotions at some point. The difference between those with this personality disorder and those without is that those without this disorder will get over the emotions within a few days or so. On the other hand, those with this disorder will have really severe forms of the problem and they will repeat over and over during a long period of time rather than just showing up and then going away shortly after. These symptoms are also going to be disrupting the lives of those with the disorder because they are so severe and occur so often.

There are a lot of issues that can arise when you are dealing with this kind of personality disorder. The issue that a lot of people have, which will be discussed a bit later in a following chapter, is that a lot of these symptoms will match up with other issues and other personality disorders. This can make it difficult sometimes to diagnose who has this kind of personality disorder and who might have another issue that is unknown. Some of the issues that you should watch out for when you are worried that someone is suffering from this kind of personality disorder include:

- Intense mood swings and emotions. These can show up in several ways. First the person may have something that they can be upset about, but the amount that they react to it is way out of line for what should be called for. They will do this all of the time instead of just once and it really can't be explained away with they are having a bad day. Other times, there may be absolutely no cause for the intense mood swings and the person will just be extremely happy one minute, angry the next, sad the next, and so on.

- Impulsive and harmful behaviors—the person with this kind of personality disorder is going to enjoy going out and seeking some thrills, no matter how dangerous these tasks may be to them or to someone else. They might go out and perform reckless driving, have risky sex, spend a lot of money that they do not have all of the time, binge eat, and abuse various forms of substance abuse. These people are not thinking about the consequences that might occur with their actions and are only worried about the moment that they are having right then.

- Issues with their relationship—most of the people with personality disorders like this one are going to have issues with their personal relationships. It really does not matter with what part of their lives and they may not have close friends or family either. This is often due to the fact that the person with this kind of personality disorder is only going to see things as good or bad and they will not see things differently or that others have opinions that are valid and different from their own. Also, the opinion that they have of someone else is going to dramatically change over any little thing. At one minute they may think you guys are best friends, but the next you may have to back out of a date or a meeting because of your kids at home, and the person with the personality disorder will start to see you as bad and want nothing to do with you. This makes it almost impossible for them to have relationships with anyone.

- Low self-worth—the reason for this is not fully understood but it could be because they have no one whom they can be close to or because the chemicals in the brain that are responsible for this part of their lives are not working properly. These people are going to feel a lot of the time that they are not worth anyone paying attention to them and they might wonder why anyone would want to be their friend. This can make it difficult to talk to them because they are not going to see the point and may not have a lot to say.

- A fear that is almost frantic of being abandoned or left alone—since this person is dealing with a low self-worth and does not have many relationships that are working well for them, they may fear that the few friends whom they do have are not going to be there when they need them. The person with this disorder may start to do things that are considered frantic to hold onto the ones who may be close to them. On the other end of the spectrum, they may also reject and push away others because they feel it is better to do this before the ones they love can do it to them.

- Aggressive behavior—remember with this that the person with the disorder is going through some intense moments at the time and they are not sure of who they can trust of what they should be doing. These mixed up emotions are going to cause them to act out in ways that are not common for the general populace. Many people with borderline personality disorder are going to exhibit this kind of aggressive behavior.

- Feeling alone and empty inside—this can be two-fold. First, the person is going to feel this way because their emotions are all over and they do not feel like they are worth anything. The few people who are around them may make the person feel like they are not worthy of love so they will push them away. In addition, since the person is not able to hold onto relationships all that well, they may have some issues with feeling alone because they have no one who is there to help them out.

- Problems with violence and anger—in some cases you may think that you are dealing with a little child who has never been told the word no. This is because the person with the personality disorder is prone to getting very angry and since they do not know how to control or express the anger, it is going to erupt in some temper tantrums that can be violent. It is not that they are trying to act like a little child, it is more that they are not sure how to act in society and much like a little child, they just explode with emotions that they do not understand and do not know what to do with.

- Hurting themselves—often those with borderline personality disorder will resort to causing themselves physical harm. This would include things such as burning or cutting themselves. This is going to be a repeat issues, but it may be hard to see because the person is going to be working to hide up the scars so that no one else is able to see what is going on. For example, they may wear long dress shirts, long pants, and refuse to be anywhere that a lot of skin would be showing, such as a swimming pool.

- Suicide attempts as well as suicidal thoughts—this is not uncommon in someone with borderline personality disorder. These thoughts stem from their risky behavior, trouble with emotions, and the fact that they feel all alone in this world.

- Paranoia and losing touch with reality—the human mind is a social creature. It likes to be around others that it can have conversations with, laugh with and have a good time. Doing this is kind of hard for the person with this kind of disorder. They always feel like they are alone and often they are the ones who destroy the relationships that they are in. This leaves them with very few options when it comes to being social with others. As a result, their brains may turn a bit against them, over time, and they may begin to feel like others are after them or that they are not quite in touch with their reality like they should be.

As you can see, a lot of these symptoms are the same ones that you will be able to find in other personality disorders. This is what makes it really difficult to figure out if you have this kind of disorder and which kind you may have if not. It is never a good idea to diagnose yourself or someone else with this kind of personality disorder because you could be wrong and then the wrong treatments are given. It is much better to visit a doctor if there is a possibility of this disorder being present so that the person with it can get the help that they need quickly.

Chapter 3 Communicating with the Borderline

One of the biggest concerns with Borderline Personality Disorders is how you, as a person with BPD, can form healthy relationships with someone and vice versa. We all want someone we can say 'I love you' to, to be happy with the people around us, to have good working relationships with our coworkers, and to perform well in a job we just started working in.

For people who have BPD, life can be challenging. There are intense feelings of anger, desperation, strong emotional pain, feelings of emptiness, and hopelessness and it can also make you feel lonely very often. It's like looking inside a happy home and wishing you were part of it or floating, looking down at people who are happy and wishing you can feel what they feel. Loneliness, desperation, anger, strong and intense emotional pain are all symptoms that can affect every piece of your life. Many people with BPD learn to cope despite these challenges and they work hard to live fulfilling lives.

In this chapter, we will focus on the most crucial segments of life-relationships and the workplace and how it impacts a person with BPD. For children who have yet to be diagnosed or who are already diagnosed with BPD, if left untreated, these could be the struggles that they may go through.

This chapter opens your mind as a parent to the future possibility of what your child may have to go through as they grow older. Hopefully, it will also nudge you towards getting early diagnosis and intervention for your child and emotional support for yourself as a parent. This chapter also endeavors to help adults with and without BPD on how they can manage relationships.

Who are the Ones with Borderline Personality Disorder?

When you read about Borderline Personality Disorder, you may have come across plenty of articles talking about trauma. This is because plenty of people diagnosed with BPD have gone through some form of trauma in their lives. It could also be genetics that plays a role in people developing Borderline Personality Disorder. Research and studies show that if you have a parent, a sibling or a child with BPD, the chances are that you developing it is five times possible. Neurological impairment also seems to be an element that causes BPD, which means in some areas of your brain, there are no proper communication pathways that exist the way a typical brain works.

In many cases, borderline personality disorder begins in adolescence or the latest, young adulthood, and it is estimated that at least 1.6 percent of adolescents deal with BPD. This number could be higher because some cases or people go undiagnosed or untreated. It is also reported that females are generally diagnosed with BPD, but studies have also shown that males tend to be misdiagnosed with either depression or PTSD instead of BPD.

BPD and its Impact on Family

Mental illness, whether it's just you have it, or your child, or your partner or just someone in your family, like your sibling has it it affects the entire family unit. The older the person gets, the more complicated the symptoms can be.

Where personality disorders are concerned, this effect is severe because of the intrinsic impairments that exist in interpersonal relationships. The most affected are partners and family members of the PBD individual as they are the closest and most often in touch. They also have a high impact on the person who has this disorder in return.

There are very limited therapeutic options available for family members of those with BPD. Among the reasons are that there are limited research and studies done on families.

These 5 criteria have been established by the Diagnostic and Statically Manual of Mental Disorders IV. BRD rates range from 0.07 to two percent, which means that there are millions of families out there who are affected as well.

Family members usually play the role of caregiver or case manager. Apart from this, stereotypes and conventional gender roles are the main drivers for women in the household to take up the major responsibility of caring for the individual with BPD. Family members may also field suicidal behavior, a task that crisis prevention and intervention workers are trained and paid to do.

Risks of Depression

Studies that have been done on family members with BPD relatives have shown that they too, suffer the side effects of BPD, primarily depression. A relative with a mental illness also causes family members or primary caregivers to suffer grief, isolation, and burden because of the stress of having to deal with a person with BPD. This also relates to parents who care for children and adolescents with BPD.

Among the biggest aggressors for mental health providers were suicide attempts, patient anger as well as threats of suicide. These three elements are all characteristics of BPD and have a substantial impact on loved ones.

According to observations conducted by researchers Hoffman and Gunderson, families are equally distressed by the exact problems that mental health professionals have, and these problems are, in fact, more demoralizing for families more than the healthcare provider. Families can be severely overwhelmed that they, too, have trouble in managing the symptoms of their loved ones with BPD. What is even more distressing is that family members are not trained for the role of caregiver and usually must learn skills of managing symptoms alongside the PBD adult or child.

Psychological Impact on Families

The impact of BPD psychologically on loved ones cannot be ignored. At times, family members can also feel traumatized, which also confines their emotional responses to be of any help to the BPD individual. Based on reports by the Center for Disease Control and Prevention, the average suicide attempts by a BPD adult are 3.4 times during their lifetime and at least 73 percent of people diagnosed with BPD have attempted suicide at least once in their lives. Unfortunately, an overwhelming 10% of individuals with BPD have committed suicide.

Stress on Families

No doubt that BPD puts an entire family under significant stress, and this level of stress differs differently from parent to a sibling, child to parent and sibling to sibling. The person with BPD has unpredictable behavior and sometimes it just lasts for a few hours but sometimes it can go on for days.

Symptoms are extremely, and triggers are many. The family unit can gain better insight and support from other parental groups, mental health groups, as well as family counseling, family therapy, and advisory groups. Without support, it is practically impossible to deal with a child or adult with BPD.

Families can help ease and calm the loved one with BPD, and the role that families play in the life of the PBD individual is extremely important in helping them manage their condition at home.

Another stress factor for families is the inability to find the right care and therapist it often takes very long to find a good one and even longer to find the one that connects with the patient, makes them feel validated, understood and not judged.

Positive and Negatives of Receiving Diagnosis Family Point of View

The positive aspects of receiving a diagnosis are that when you do, you can seek the right treatment, find the right therapy for both the individual with BPD as well as for caregivers. DBT is one such treatment that we will explore in another chapter it is an extremely helpful therapy that is being practiced more commonly now than before. Other psychological therapies are also available but getting a psychologist that specializes in CBT may not necessarily be the right choice.

It is vital for someone who knows about this condition to treat BPD because it can get very bad, very quickly, and get the correct treatment as soon as possible for the adult, adolescent, or child is imperative. The other good thing about getting a diagnosis is that, through the right treatment, self-harm can be stopped and by extension, suicidal attempts.

The negative aspect of receiving a diagnosis is that BPD is an extremely misunderstood condition, which often comes with its very own stigmatization among people in the community and society at large. However, getting a diagnosis far outweighs this negative aspect. In many ways, it is important not to judge a person no matter how difficult their behavior is because we do not know what they are going through. The family concerned, especially parents, should not be judged as well.

Family Support for a BPD Child or Adult

For parents, one of the best ways to support a child or adolescent with BPD is to make sure they go for their treatments. Parents are encouraged to go for parent-run groups and workshops that help educate family members in convenient and useful ways to help a child cope with BPD. Among the knowledge shared are coping skills as well as strategies to aid someone when they go through any impulsivity or behavioral changes as well as gain a better understanding of the illness. Workshops and support groups also teach parents how to navigate a child with difficult BPD behaviors before they can turn extreme.

The psychologist treating the child or adult will also request that they meet as a family group to explain things, symptoms, and actions. Above all, education is necessary and a vital tool to support the family who, in turn, can better support the individual with BPD.

Support from Mental Health Care Providers

The therapist, psychologist, or doctor is generally the first person who the family contacts if someone is not mentally well. Families have the responsibility of informing the doctor or psychologist about what the individual goes through, what symptoms do they have, any episodes of meltdowns and basically everything that the adult or child experiences. Talking about family history is also vital.

A psychologist that is trained in BPD will be able to talk to the individual in a compassionate way and get them to take their medication and vitamins as well as organize for referrals and evaluations through the period of treatment. The psychologist would also be able to draw up a mental health plan and some sedatives (even if the diagnosis has not been established) to help manage immediate issues concerning the BPD individual, such as anxiety and insomnia.

The right doctor or psychologist will also be able to see the patient as often as possible and talk about ways to get through their episodes and cope with whatever symptoms that kept arising. If symptoms get worse, a psychiatrist or doctor will recommend that the individual admit themselves in the hospital which will also lead to correct diagnosis done. It is extremely important to stay in touch with a doctor that is clear, understanding, direct and above all, non-judgmental.

Doctors, psychologists, and therapists are trained to answer questions from BPD individuals or any individual with a mental disorder.

Impact on Relationships

According to DSM-5, which is the resource material that mental health professionals refer to when making any diagnosis, the intensity of emotions, unstableness as well as conflicted personal relationships are the main manifestations of BPD. At times, there can also be sudden shifts of feelings from feeling smothered to feeling fearful which leads individuals with BPD to withdraw or cling to relationships.

This back and forth innuendo of feelings are stressful for both the partner and the BPD individual. Another impact of BPD is abandonment sensitivity. This sensitivity causes BPD individuals to be constantly watching out for signs that their partners will leave them, and they decipher even minor issues, arguments, or events as signs of their partners leaving them. As a result, the BPD individual acts out in frantic measures to prevent abandonment from causing public scenes, pleading, and even to go so far as to physically prevent them from leaving even if their partners never intended to.

Lying is another complaint partner must deal with in BPD relationships. Deception and lying are not the formal criteria of BPD diagnosis, but there are reports and feedback given from partners saying that lying is a major concern in their relationships because BPD people see things from a different set of lenses.

When it comes to relationships, impulsive sexuality is also another common symptom of BPD. BPD individuals struggle with sexuality as a large percentage of them have experienced some form of sexual abuse as a child, which has sex and sexual relations with their partners complex and complicated.

Self-harm, dissociative symptoms, and impulsivity also make up a large component of BPD symptoms in relationships, which causes major stress among partners. A person with BPD may engage in impulsive tendencies such as binge drinking, fast driving, going on extreme spending sprees, which impact the relationship in both financial and emotional aspects. Suicidal tendencies also present extremely scary episodes for romantic partners who do not want to see the individual get hurt. All these cause extreme stress, depression and anxiety on the partner without BPD.

What does Research tell us about Romantic Relationships and BPD?

A stormy and unpredictable romantic relationship is often the case when it comes to people with BPD. These relationships are distinguished by a great deal of dysfunction and turmoil. It's hard to say that the BDP person has control over things, and it is also to tell their partner without BPD to be extremely understanding. It is like a push and pull game all the time.

When it comes to relationships, it's as complex and complicated. For example, women with BPD symptoms have reported having higher chronic relationship stress and were involved in more frequent fights. Studies have also pointed out that the more serious a person's BPD symptoms are, the less satisfied they are in their relationships. Research has also stated that BPD symptoms relate to a higher number of romantic relationships over a period as well as greater incidences of unplanned pregnancies. Individuals with BPD also have more former partners and shorter romantic relationships than people without any personality disorders. This also suggests that romantic relationships with someone who has BPD has a higher chance of ending up in a breakup or divorce.

Where sex is concerned, research also states that BPD women have more negative perceptions about sex, more uncertain about sex than women without BPD, and are more likely to feel pressured into having sex with their partners. There is very little research done on men with BPD and sexuality. The worst part is watching yourself destroy relationships, knowing that you're doing it as it's happening and not being able to stop it.

Starting a Romantic Relationship with Someone Who Has BPD

Would anyone want to start a relationship with a person who has BPD, given that there are all these complexities and difficulties that exist? A relationship with two typical, non-BPD individuals is complicated, what more one with BPD in the mix?

Firstly, it is vital to keep in mind that despite the disruptive and intense symptoms, people with BPD are like everyone one they are kind, they are good, and they are caring individuals who want the best for their partners. There are plenty of good and positive qualities about them that make them a great partner to be with. Partners who are in relationships with someone who has BPD have said how they are fun, passionate, and exciting. For many people who are in relationships with a BPD partner, they are drawn to the intense emotions and strong desires for intimacy.

Am I able to make a romantic BPD relationship last?

Like most relationships, a BPD relationship also has its honeymoon period where everything is wonderful and blissful. BPD individuals have said that at the beginning of a new romantic relationships, they form an idealization of their partners, often placing their partner in high esteem, as if they have no faults, feeling like they have found the perfect soulmate, a perfect match, the right person who will rescue them from their emotional distress.

The honeymoon period exists with the new partner too, where everything is exciting, the passion is intense, the sex great and the emotions so blissful. The idea is always the same it's nice to finally have someone who feels strongly about you and makes you feel like you are very much needed.

But then this perfect idealization begins to erode, and problems start creeping in when reality kicks in and life unravels. The person with BPD often finds that their new partner does come with flaws, and the perfect image of a soulmate comes starts breaking apart.

The issue here is that people with BPD also struggle with this issue called dichotomous thinking, which makes them see things only in black and white there is no grey area, no middle ground. Because of this, they often have problems identifying or coming to terms that people, average people, make mistakes even with well intentions.

Because of the intensity of their emotions, they are often passion swings both ways they quickly change from idealization to devaluation. To maintain relationships with a BPD partner is to find ways of coping with their turbulent cycles. The key here is also to encourage them to seek professional help to enable them to reduce these cycles. This is often what couples therapy does to help partners in BPD relationships.

How to Manage a Romantic BPD Relationship

Apart from couple's therapy, there are other therapies that need to be undergone in order to have a healthy relationship not just in romantic terms but in life as a general.

- Dialectical Behavior Therapy (DBT)

This is a form of Cognitive Behavioral Therapy which we will explore in greater detail in a separate chapter. But essentially, DBT endeavors to bridge a person's thinking to their behavior. Among the four main skills taught in DBT, managing interpersonal skills is one of them.

- Mentalization Therapy (MBT)

This type of therapy helps to align a person's thoughts and enable them to make sense of what goes on in their mind as well as the minds of the people they communicate with.

- Medications

Medications are often prescribed by doctors to enable the individual to cope with some of their symptoms. Some medications also help improve BPD symptoms, help a person manage their impulsivity, anger as well as depression.

Chapter 4 Taking Back Control of Your Life

Just like any disorder, a mental illness in the family would affect the entire unit as a whole. It has an acute effect on those with personality disorders because it affects interpersonal relationships. The impact of BPD is most felt on the families of those with the illness, an effect that also bounces back on the individual who is suffering.

Families of people with borderline personality disorder are affected in various ways. One or two people are usually designated as the case manager for their family member. It is also common to observe gender stereotyping because the women in the family, by default, are given the responsibility to take care of a family member who is sick; personality disorders included. Studies have also shown that family members of people who suffer from a mental disorder are more prone to becoming depressed. A relative with mental illness such as borderline personality disorder often has feelings of isolation and grief. Naturally, this would also result in feeling emotionally overburdened. In fact, research shows that suicide attempts and patient anger are leading causes of stress for mental health providers. These depressive symptoms are also evident in borderline personality disorder, further proving that the illness remains to have a significant effect on families and loved ones.

Family members also tend to feel overwhelmed in managing the symptoms of a relative with BPD. Additionally, they don't have the training, skills, and experience to manage it effectively while living normal lives of their own. Borderline personality disorder has a strong impact on families, and this fact should not be overlooked. Family members may end up feeling traumatized and this will make them emotionally incapable of taking care of their relative and providing any form of moral support. Statistics show that 10% of individuals with borderline personality disorder commit suicide, placing emphasis on the importance of care a person receives.

However, studies show that when family members are more emotionally engaged with their ill relative, the patient significantly improves their chances of reducing symptoms over the course of a year.

Although limited, there are therapeutic options that family members of those with borderline personality disorder can try. The primary reason behind this is that there the research on family relationships of those with BPD and other mental illnesses remains inadequate today. But given that the statistics estimate around 2 percent of the population are diagnosed with borderline personality disorder, this means that millions of family members are affected. When family members participate in counseling and programs that are designed for their own well-being, this will greatly benefit all parties involved.

Current programs that are aimed at providing support towards family members are derived from Dialectical Behavior Therapy as well as the stress coping and adaptation model. These have proven effective and should be a serious consideration for anyone who has a loved one suffering from borderline personality disorder. The stress coping and adaptation model focuses on healing based on a person's adaptive abilities, resources, and individual strengths. This leads to adaptive coping as it helps strengthen a person's way of dealing with the issue by applying both behavioral and cognitive techniques.

Dialectical behavior therapy is one of the more popular and effective methods of treating borderline personality disorder and its symptoms. This form of therapy is highly recommended for family members of those who have BPD because it focuses on change, coping strategies, and acceptance. The most effective treatment for borderline personality disorder combines teaching communication skills and coping strategies for the patient while also providing support through group networks for the family members.

Dealing with Siblings who have BPD

Sibling relationship can be multifaceted and complex at times. Usually, jealousy and competitiveness are present especially in the desire to seek approval from parents. If a sibling is diagnosed with borderline personality disorder, this may result in intense negative emotional experiences between siblings.

Children and teenagers who have BPD normally are at the receiving end of most of the attention at home. If you have a brother whose emotional behavior demanded that your parents focus more on him, this may cause you to feel resentment, jealousy, and neglect. The burden of witnessing negative behavior and the stress that your sibling's BPD symptoms has on the family also falls on you. However, when your sibling takes action to seek out treatment for BPD, it is crucial that they feel the support of the entire family including you. Working through your own feelings will be an important catalyst in changing the family dynamic, helping you and your sibling move forward for the benefit of the family unit as a whole.

Feeling angry, resentful, and jealous is normal before a sibling is treated for BPD. However, it is recognized that individuals who suffer as a result of a sibling's BPD symptoms have needs that need to be addressed too. While people with BPD need full emotional and moral support from their loved ones, their families are in need of the same things as well. Support groups focused on families of those who have BPD are an excellent place to start and will help you learn more about the disorder. Support groups will also help you work through the complex feelings you are experiencing as a result of being the affected sibling of someone who is borderline.

When facing this challenge, remember that you are not alone because many other brothers and sisters have had to deal with the trauma of growing up with a sibling who suffered from BPD. Support groups provide helpful validation of the experience as a whole and can help you see things in a new perspective. Furthermore, support groups can also teach you about effective communication techniques that you can apply when talking to a sibling who has BPD.

By educating yourself about the disorder, you can identify skills that will prove indispensable in dealing family members with BPD. More importantly you will learn how to best support your sibling at a time when they need you the most, even though they don't act like it. You will also learn to set boundaries as you empower yourself so that you will no longer feel like you are at the receiving end of your sibling's negative emotional outbursts.

Once your sibling begins treatment for borderline personality disorder, they are clearly communicating that they have invested in improving their interpersonal relationships. However, the road to recovery may be full of obstacles and oftentimes won't be easy for them. They may show signs of improvement but with certain stressors may end up taking a step back to destructive behavior. It is up to the family, siblings involved, to help them through the journey as they full recover from BPD. Providing moral support to someone who has BPD also means taking care of yourself emotionally and physically in order to give the best possible support you can.

It is also important to remember that a sibling who has BPD will not have it for life. Borderline personality disorder is a curable disorder, but the earlier it is diagnosed the more effective and successful treatment will be. Since BPD is often characterized by feelings of abandonment, depression, and feeling highly emotional, your sibling will appreciate working through the ordeal with them. Once it's all over you can expect to have a more fulfilling relationship with them.

Mothers With Borderline Personality Disorder and Its Effect on Childhood Development

Childhood is a time where both parents and child learn new things and face challenges. For the child, it is when they are most sensitive to their environment. It is when they are more vulnerable to anything that may affect their development. If a mother has borderline personality disorder, it can create an added battle to the existing trials of growing up.

The National Institute of Health states that mothers with BPD symptoms are considered high-risk caregivers because of the many psychological characteristics that usually lead to negative outcomes in their own children. People with borderline personality disorder commonly have stormy and intense relationships, and mother-child relationships are no different. Mothers may have difficulty controlling their impulses and end up being angry at their child, and may even exhibit suicidal behavior. If a child witnesses BPD symptoms in their mother, who is their primary caregiver, it reduces the opportunity for the mother and child to develop stable environments that are necessary for them to develop healthy attachments to one another. Each child will have their own ups and downs in life, in the same way that there is no such thing as the perfect mother regardless of BPD.

Mothers who suffer from borderline personality disorder should participate in treatment so that they can give their children a better chance to experience stability and security. It is their responsibility to work on getting better so that they can lay out the foundation for developing better relationships with their child. When mothers do this, they also do something that is very important: preventing borderline personality disorder from being passed down to the next generation.

It is also helpful for mothers who have BPD to be educated about child rearing. They can learn additional strategies in child development while coping with the illness. Mindfulness based strategies are ideal so they can continue to be a source of warmth while monitoring their child.

Dialectical Behavior Therapy provides mothers with the emotional awareness and mindfulness skills that they need to be more effective at child rearing. Mothers who have BPD should seek help in treatment centers who have a strong focus on Dialectical Behavior Therapy so they can recover from their symptoms.

Dealing with Parents Who Have Borderline Personality Disorder

If one of your parents has BPD, you may have had a challenging upbringing. When a parent has BPD it may oftentimes have a negative effect on their children although this is not always the case. Unfortunately, it can have a serious impact on the emotions and psychological health of their child.

Children of parents who have borderline personality disorder don't have a sense of boundaries, suffer from low self-esteem, and have shame and anger issues that go on for a long time unless addressed properly. A parent who has BPD may have neglected their child's emotional, physical, or psychological needs. In extreme cases, all three of these aspects could be completely neglected. Children of those with BPD can benefit greatly from support groups designed primarily for them.

Starting the discussion with someone who has borderline personality disorder because you want them to seek help can have either positive or negative outcomes. Due to their sensitivity this kind of conversation can result in an emotional outburst. Within families, this may result in conflict and distance. People with BPD already feel that they are always being attacked, and confronting them about a mental illness could end up disastrous. The conversation will make a big difference, and should be well-thought about to reduce the chances of it going badly.

However, a parent who has never sought treatment for borderline personality disorder or who denied a diagnosis in the past may pose an added challenge. In fact they may even accuse you as the one who is mentally ill. They may put blame for many problems encountered in your own relationship. If this happens, it is best that you focus on your own healing rather than expecting the other person to change.

How to Cope With A Mother Who Has BPD

If you have a mother who has borderline personality disorder, you are most likely experiencing a difficult relationship with them. Mothers with BPD can behave erratically, ranging from insisting on being over-involved in their children's lives, or neglecting them completely.

Although your mother may not have been diagnosed with BPD, here are some symptoms that you should watch out for:

- Over-control: A common characteristic of parents with borderline personality disorder is the urge to control their children's actions, feelings, and behaviors. At times the desire to control becomes an obstacle to their child's growth and ability to develop.

- Neglect: Mothers with BPD may oftentimes be so absorbed in their seemingly overwhelming emotions that they end up neglecting their children.

Sometimes it is so severe that they are completely unable to put their child's needs before theirs.

- Criticism: Mothers with BPD are known to consistently insult or discourage their children, instead of showing them love and nurturing such as a normal mother would do. BPD mothers usually see their children as their extension, which results in the parent projecting negative feelings because it is what they see in themselves.

- Blame: Borderline mothers tend to put the blame for their sadness, anger, and frustration on their children. People with BPD have a difficult time being accountable for their actions and emotions.

Children who are raised by borderline mothers can develop numerous emotional issues as they grow older. They find it more difficult to overcome the hurtful past experienced with the BPD parent and oftentimes need to seek professional help in moving on.

If you are a child of a mother with BPD, you may experience low self-esteem, depression, or anger. The first step towards healing is to recognize that your mother's behavior is not your fault. In order to move forward it is also ideal to talk to family, friends, support groups, and even therapists who can provide moral support. Releasing your feelings in safe places will allow you to validate your own emotions and get rid of pain. There are also many ways you can change the dynamic of your relationship with your mother. It is possible to learn how to create boundaries and help yourself reduce feelings of obligation as well as guilt.

Does BPD Run in the Family?

Many parents with borderline personality disorder worry about passing it on to their children. While it is possible that your children may develop BPD later in life, it is not a guarantee because many BPD parents can learn how to raise their children and allow them to live a healthy life without inheriting the illness.

Some studies show that borderline personality disorder can run in families but there are many factors that contribute to this. Because genetics is a suspected cause of BPD, there is a small chance that your biological children can inherit certain genes from you making them more vulnerable to developing BPD.

More importantly, the kind of environment your child lives in has a greater impact in determining if they will develop borderline personality disorder. For example, if your BPD symptoms cause you to harm your child, this makes them more prone to it because they have been caused harm and possibly trauma. It can be challenging to be an effective parent if you have BPD.

While nothing can be done about genetics, parents with BPD have more control about ensuring that their children have a healthy, happy home to reduce the environmental factors that contribute to the disorder. The kind of environment a child lives in can influence the occurrence of BPD more than any other known factor.

If you are a parent with borderline personality disorder, the most important task you need to do is to ensure you are getting proper treatment. Being under the guidance of a mental health professional or therapist can greatly improve your condition which will benefit your parenting skills as well. In fact, after the first round of treatment many people are no longer considered diagnosed with borderline personality disorder. When you have less symptoms to deal with you will be able to focus on becoming a better parent.

During the course of your treatment, you should be open about asking questions to your therapist. They may be able to assist in evaluating the current home environment, and assess if your parenting skills are affected by BPD. They could also provide you with better resources such as referring you to a program that provides training and coping mechanisms for parents dealing with BPD. Depending on the severity of the illness, some parents with BPD can still turn out to be nurturing and effective although for others it takes some time.

How To Help Your Child Deal With BPD in College

Borderline personality disorder results in highly unstable emotions which can be an obstacle at being successful in school.

Managing the symptoms of BPD is crucial so that your child can reach their educational goals. As a parent there are things you can do to help your child cope with BPD and even support them in attaining one or more degrees.

Talk to your child about learning how to cope with stress whenever possible. College and university life can be a high-stress environment where seemingly simple things such as waking up early each day to go to class, making the time to study, and performing exceptionally well can place a strain on children with BPD. Living with BPD also means that one has a more difficult time dealing with stress as compared to their peers. While other schoolmates may perceive stress as a normal part of life in higher education, your child may be overwhelmed simply because they have BPD.

Although the stressors cannot be changed, you can help your child manage them better. Be supportive if they prefer to take on a smaller work load per semester, take online courses, or be a nontraditional student so that they can focus on work with less stress each day. Emphasize the importance of getting adequate sleep and proper nutrition which will be important sources of energy especially with all the studying that they need to do. Your child may also benefit from healthy social connections found in school groups as well as their own family and friends, so you can encourage them to make friends that will aid in alleviating the burden of higher education.

While most children see going away to college as the norm, a child with BPD may feel comfortable studying in a location that is closer to home. Be supportive if they feel this way because their home support system is crucial to them. If your child feels lonely this can worsen the symptoms of BPD by provoking fear of abandonment and other symptoms.

How To Help Your Loved One Start Their Career

Many kids will soon face graduation and along with that comes some daunting questions about major life decisions. If your child is one of them and is suffering from borderline personality disorder, your support will be crucial to their success in the real world.

While these major life decisions can be challenging to anyone, people with BPD may face this with more fear and anxiety than others. This is because they need to be strong in the event of being rejected from a job they have been wanting, be more determined and focused, and make new friends at their new jobs. Remember that individuals with borderline personality disorder already suffer from these symptoms:

- Intense fear of rejection

- Disturbed sense of identity

- Anxiety

- Impulsivity

- Difficulty maintaining stable relationships

Not everyone who has borderline personality disorder will struggle with starting their career. But for others the challenge can be lifelong and oftentimes paralyzing. As parents, you have to be realistic in helping your child succeed. Discuss career goals with children but keep in mind that it takes time, so it is best to avoid putting too much pressure on them because they are dealing with BPD. Since they tend to see everything in black and white they also usually have an all or nothing attitude towards events, people, and situations. If a job interview did not go well they may end up convincing themselves that they made the wrong decision or that they may never find a job at all. Help them realize that there are steps to succeeding and that one rejection doesn't mean they will fail.

Help your child concentrate on making small steps towards reaching their goals. If they focus on only one major goal this can be frustrating and will cause them to give up. Have them focus on small accomplishments that will not only help them move forward but that will also help them to feel good. Encourage them to focus their efforts on sending out at least 5 job applications a day to better improve their chances at landing a job. When they do accomplish these goals, celebrate with them. The moral support lent by parents, family, and friends mean the world to people with borderline personality disorder.

It is also important for parents to keep their cool regardless of the outcome of a job interview. Whether it is positive or negative, be supportive of your child. Recognize their success and also empathize with them if they are dealing with failure or rejection. When talking to your child about the outcome of a job interview or their first day at work, use an even tone of voice that will ensure your support and care for them regardless of their performance at the job. If they find that the learning curve is difficult, provide concrete ways of helping them learn what they need to do in order to work better. For example, they may feel completely in the dark about how to create professional emails and proposals. Sit down with them and teach them how to write emails but encourage them to be independent in seeking resources and information that will help them learn.

Encourage them to keep a routine which will help them stay sane despite what feels like crazy days when one is in the midst of building their career. By having a strong, healthy routine in place it will give them more control. Help them create a routine that works for them, such as certain times of the day that are dedicated to job searches, sending out applications, and making phone calls. It is just as important to ensure that they have a time in the day that they can step away from the job hunt and instead focus on themselves, engaging in activities that make them feel good such as spending time with friends or participating in their favorite hobby.

When young people with borderline personality disorder are just starting out their career, the support of family and friends can make the difference from success and failure. If the symptoms of BPD make it difficult for them to starting or keeping a job, treatment is needed. Once the symptoms are under control they can start their career on the right foot. In fact, many borderline personality disorder treatment centers also offer vocational assistance which can also help your loved one in creating a resume, starting the job hunt, and coaching for interviews. Effective Treatments and Therapies for Borderline Personality Disorder

Borderline Personality disorder can be a scary condition-no one wants to be stuck with someone who is so unstable for the rest of their lives.

But you don't have to because it is not a permanent condition. Many people stick with the condition for longer than usual only because they couldn't identify that there is a problem and get a diagnosis early enough.

Once your loved one has been diagnosed, there are a lot of therapies and treatments that can help them improve and start to get better immediately.

Some of the effective treatments and therapies for Borderline Personality Disorder include:

Psychotherapy

Psychotherapy for Borderline Personality Disorder is also known as Talk Therapy. It involves the use of interpersonal or group interaction to try to change a person's behaviors and teach them better ways to interact with other people and handle the challenges they face with their moods, self-image, and thought process.

There are a lot of psychotherapy methods that are used to treat Borderline Personality Disorder but the most effective ones include:

☐ Dialectal Behavior Therapy

Dialectal Behavior Therapy also known as DBT, is a psychotherapy that helps to teach the patient healthy ways to cope with stress, manage conflicts, regulate their emotions, and improve their relationships.

It can also help to prevent destructive behaviors and eating disorders in people suffering from BPD.

Dialectal Behavior therapy was first introduced in the late 80's by Dr. Mashan Linehan, after discovering that Cognitive Behavioral Therapy(CBT), which commonly worked for people suffering from other personality disorders, was not effective for people suffering from Borderline Personality Disorder.

Dialectal Behavior Therapy is based on the concept of Dialectics, which is a belief that for every force, there is an opposing force that is stronger.

Patients are made to understand that:

- Change is inevitable and constant

- Everything is connected

- Opposing forces can come together to bring out positive results

People who suffer from BPD often have problems dealing with changes and opposing ideas, actions or personalities so this therapy teaches them how to embrace and manage changes, and help them to see that change is inevitable and an inherent quality of life itself.

Patients are also taught how to validate other people's opinions and ideas without necessarily accepting that it is the best approach.

Rather than throw tantrums because you said that Pizza is a better dinner than burger, they would be able to 'respect' your opposing ideas and opinions without necessarily accepting or adopting it.

Dialectal Behavior therapy is one of the most effective treatments for Borderline Personality Disorder and it is often done through group sessions, phone coaching and one on one therapy.

☐ Schema-Focused Therapy (SCT)

Schema-focused therapy helps patients to identify negative behaviors and patterns that they might have developed over time as a coping skill for Borderline Personality Disorder.

For instance, an adult who has suffered from BPD from when they were a child could have developed some negative traits like maybe binge-eating or snapping at people or being too clingy in order to prevent people from abandoning them.

Schema-focused therapy helps to identify these negative coping skills, and helps the patient to learn new, positive coping skills.

☐ Mentalization-based Therapy (MBT)

Another therapy that teaches BPD patients positive coping skills is Mentalization-based Therapy.

Patients are taught how to chart their own thoughts and feelings, and identify what they may be feeling at any point in time so that they can properly ponder on issues before reacting.

BPD patients are prone to impulsive habits and actions-they often react before they think unlike the rest of us who would often think about our actions and reactions carefully before letting them out.

Mentalization-based therapy basically helps patients to think and reflect on the consequeces of their actions before acting them out.

□ Transference-focused Psychotherapy (TFP)

Transference-focused psychotherapy is really great for BPD patients who are married or in romantic relationship, and want to improve their relationship with their partner.

The psychotherapist teaches the patient how to understand their emotions and develop good interpersonal relationship that the patient can duplicate with other people.

All of these therapies are effective and patients can choose one or a combination of therapies depending on what their problem areas are.

However, you would need the help of a mental healthcare professional or a psychologist to recommend the best therapy for the individual.

- Medications: Drugs like antidepressants, mood stabilizers, and antipsychotics are very helpful too especially for reducing symptoms like depression, anxiety, aggressiveness, and impulsiveness.

A doctor can prescribe medications to be used along with therapy because medications alone may only have temporary effects while a combination of both can provide permanent relief from Borderline Personality Disorder.

- Hospitalization: Hospitalization may be necessary where the patient may be suicidal or engaging in self-harm. They would have to be hospitalized and placed on suicide watch where they can start to take medications and therapies that would help to improve their condition.

- Self-help: There are a lot of ways that a person suffering from Borderline Personality Disorder can help themselves outside medications and therapies.

Some helpful self-help strategies include:

- Breathing Exercises: Breathing exercises help you calm down by sending signals to your sympathetic nervous system that is responsible for coordinating your flight or fight response.

Learning how to breathe, especially during distressful situations can help to prevent interpersonal conflicts.

Instead of responding impulsively, the patient can cultivate a habit of taking quick, deep breaths before responding to any situation.

It will not only help them calm down, but also help them ponder on actions before acting them out.

- Journaling and Mood-charting: The brain of a person with Borderline Personality Disorder can be likened to that of a little child. A little child is yet to understand why they are feeling a certain way, and they can't express their feelings so they would cry, throw tantrums and lash out all the time.

But if the child is able to identify what he or she is feeling at that moment, they can easily say "I'm hungry' rather than cry until you ask them if they want food.

Mood-charting can help a patient anticipate and identify their feelings at any point in time, so that they can avoid 'punishing' other people instead of looking inwards and tackling the issue from within them.

Mood-charting can be done with a pocket notebook, where the patient would have to record their moods and feelings at every hour of the day for a period of time, maybe a couple of weeks or months.

After some time, a pattern would emerge and it will be easy to tell how and what the patient may feel at different periods.

The patient would also be able to prepare themselves to handle the people and challenges that they are likely to come across during these periods.

- Family Therapy

The truth is that it is the family and friends that suffer most. If you are living with someone who suffers from BPD, it can take a negative toll on you and since the condition can be passed on to people who grew up or lived with BPD patients for a long time, your children may be at risk of developing Borderline Personality disorder too.

Family therapy is not only helpful for learning how to cope with, and live with patients without conflicts, it can also be a preventive or protective measure for people who have to live with or relate with a person who has the Borderline Personality Disorder.

Family therapy involves all members of the household working together with a therapist. You would all attend sessions as a group, where you would be taught how to communicate and cope with the patient, and how to avoid dangerous BPD family cycles from forming.

You would also be taught how to set boundaries and take care of yourself while caring for your loved one.

Family therapy is often more effective than individual therapy because the patient will still face difficulties at home if family and friends don't know how to communicate and live with them until their condition improves.

There are a lot of family therapy programs for Borderline Personality Disorder but a very common and effective one is Systems Training for Emotional Predictability and Problem-solving (STEPPS). It is a 20-week program that all family members have to attend. The program helps you learn how to predict the patient's reactions to common issues, and help you learn positive ways to respond, communicate and live with them.

Recovery Takes Time

Your loved one will get better as soon as they start receiving treatments but it is important to note that this will not happen overnight.

Some patients will get better almost immediately, while some might take years to respond to recovery so make sure you are patient with your loved one, and you give them as much time as they need to get better.

Chapter 5 BPD and Successful Treatment

All along, we've been talking about how to take care of your partner who has Borderline Personality Disorder but what about you?

Borderline Personality Disorder definitely takes its toll on the partner and family members. In fact, you are the ones who bear the brunt in the relationship because you have to be the bigger one all the time.

You have to ignore a lot of things and be emotionally strong because a lot of what your partner does can hurt you and drive you crazy.

So how do you take care of yourself to ensure that you don't lose it while living with, and loving a person who has Borderline Personality Disorder?

Understand Some of the Ways That Their Illness Can Affect You, and Be Prepared for Them

The first key to caring for yourself is anticipating the difficulties. It's easier to deal with the issues when you already expect or know what would happen.

Living with a person who has Borderline Personality Disorder can affect the partner and the family in a number of ways including:

1.   Disruption in Regular Routines

Their mood is hardly stable and so are their desires. You could have planned to attend a family event together during the weekend and when the day comes, your partner decides that they want to stay back at home to watch soccer, or they would rather spend the day with a friend instead.

All of this is bound to get to you, and make you really angry because, how do you tell your mom and dad that he's no longer coming? And for what? Because he wants to hang out with a random stranger instead?

The truth is that, when dealing with someone who has the borderline personality disorder, you have to be flexible, both in your expectations of them, and in what you tell others that they would do.

Even when your partner has promised and swears that they would do something, always have it at the back of your mind that it's possible that they won't be able to do it, not because they don't want to, but because they have a temporary illness that prevents them from taking full control of their actions and decisions.

2.   Financial Difficulties

Impulsive behaviors are common with people who suffer from this disorder and impulsive spending is one of the most challenging of their impulsive tendencies.

Your partner can make a mess of the family's finances if they are given total control. You may soon find yourself dealing with a lot of debt repayments due to financial recklessness on your partner's part.

Whilst it may be difficult for you to ask your partner not to do whatever they like with their own money, you can encourage them to use a budget to plan expenditure.

A budget can go a long way in preventing impulsive spending.

3. Changes in Traditional Family Roles

Another problem you may experience in the relationship is the frequent changes in family roles.

Traditionally, the man is like the head or the authority figure in the home-he protects his family, makes decisions and basically, takes charge of the home. The woman on the other hand, is the one who cooks the meals, tends to the household, and takes care of the kids, and so on.

Not trying to be misogynistic here but these are the traditional roles in most households.

But when dealing with a person who has the disorder, you can find yourself switching roles, and standing in for them a lot of times.

She may wake up one morning and decide that she doesn't want to get out of bed that day while she is supposed to be the one who preps the kids for school. So, you would have to step in and fulfill her responsibilities for that day.

A child who has a parent that has Borderline Personality Disorder might find themselves being the caretaker and decision maker a lot of times whereas, it's usually the other way round.

You have to be prepared for these traditional role reversals so as to keep the family functioning; otherwise, the family may become dysfunctional.

Chapter 6 What Is Your BPD Type

Borderline Personality disorder can be a scary condition-no one wants to be stuck with someone who is so unstable for the rest of their lives.

But you don't have to because it is not a permanent condition. Many people stick with the condition for longer than usual only because they couldn't identify that there is a problem and get a diagnosis early enough.

Once your loved one has been diagnosed, there are a lot of therapies and treatments that can help them improve and start to get better immediately.

Some of the effective treatments and therapies for Borderline Personality Disorder include:

Psychotherapy

Psychotherapy for Borderline Personality Disorder is also known as Talk Therapy. It involves the use of interpersonal or group interaction to try to change a person's behaviors and teach them better ways to interact with other people and handle the challenges they face with their moods, self-image, and thought process.

There are a lot of psychotherapy methods that are used to treat Borderline Personality Disorder but the most effective ones include:

☐ Dialectal Behavior Therapy

Dialectal Behavior Therapy also known as DBT, is a psychotherapy that helps to teach the patient healthy ways to cope with stress, manage conflicts, regulate their emotions, and improve their relationships.

It can also help to prevent destructive behaviors and eating disorders in people suffering from BPD.

Dialectal Behavior therapy was first introduced in the late 80's by Dr. Mashan Linehan, after discovering that Cognitive Behavioral Therapy(CBT), which commonly worked for people suffering from other personality disorders, was not effective for people suffering from Borderline Personality Disorder.

Dialectal Behavior Therapy is based on the concept of Dialectics, which is a belief that for every force, there is an opposing force that is stronger.

Patients are made to understand that:

- Change is inevitable and constant
- Everything is connected
- Opposing forces can come together to bring out positive results

People who suffer from BPD often have problems dealing with changes and opposing ideas, actions or personalities so this therapy teaches them how to embrace and manage changes, and help them to see that change is inevitable and an inherent quality of life itself.

Patients are also taught how to validate other people's opinions and ideas without necessarily accepting that it is the best approach.

Rather than throw tantrums because you said that Pizza is a better dinner than burger, they would be able to 'respect' your opposing ideas and opinions without necessarily accepting or adopting it.

Dialectal Behavior therapy is one of the most effective treatments for Borderline Personality Disorder and it is often done through group sessions, phone coaching and one on one therapy.

☐ Schema-Focused Therapy (SCT)

Schema-focused therapy helps patients to identify negative behaviors and patterns that they might have developed over time as a coping skill for Borderline Personality Disorder.

For instance, an adult who has suffered from BPD from when they were a child could have developed some negative traits like maybe binge-eating or snapping at people or being too clingy in order to prevent people from abandoning them.

Schema-focused therapy helps to identify these negative coping skills, and helps the patient to learn new, positive coping skills.

☐ Mentalization-based Therapy (MBT)

Another therapy that teaches BPD patients positive coping skills is Mentalization-based Therapy.

Patients are taught how to chart their own thoughts and feelings, and identify what they may be feeling at any point in time so that they can properly ponder on issues before reacting.

BPD patients are prone to impulsive habits and actions-they often react before they think unlike the rest of us who would often think about our actions and reactions carefully before letting them out.

Mentalization-based therapy basically helps patients to think and reflect on the consequences of their actions before acting them out.

☐ Transference-focused Psychotherapy (TFP)

Transference-focused psychotherapy is really great for BPD patients who are married or in romantic relationship, and want to improve their relationship with their partner.

The psychotherapist teaches the patient how to understand their emotions and develop good interpersonal relationship that the patient can duplicate with other people.

All of these therapies are effective and patients can choose one or a combination of therapies depending on what their problem areas are.

However, you would need the help of a mental healthcare professional or a psychologist to recommend the best therapy for the individual.

- Medications: Drugs like antidepressants, mood stabilizers, and antipsychotics are very helpful too especially for reducing symptoms like depression, anxiety, aggressiveness, and impulsiveness.

A doctor can prescribe medications to be used along with therapy because medications alone may only have temporary effects while a combination of both can provide permanent relief from Borderline Personality Disorder.

- Hospitalization: Hospitalization may be necessary where the patient may be suicidal or engaging in self-harm. They would have to be hospitalized and placed on suicide watch where they can start to take medications and therapies that would help to improve their condition.

- Self-help: There are a lot of ways that a person suffering from Borderline Personality Disorder can help themselves outside medications and therapies.

Some helpful self-help strategies include:

- Breathing Exercises: Breathing exercises help you calm down by sending signals to your sympathetic nervous system that is responsible for coordinating your flight or fight response.

Learning how to breathe, especially during distressful situations can help to prevent interpersonal conflicts.

Instead of responding impulsively, the patient can cultivate a habit of taking quick, deep breaths before responding to any situation.

It will not only help them calm down, but also help them ponder on actions before acting them out.

- Journaling and Mood-charting: The brain of a person with Borderline Personality Disorder can be likened to that of a little child. A little child is yet to understand why they are feeling a certain way, and they can't express their feelings so they would cry, throw tantrums and lash out all the time.

But if the child is able to identify what he or she is feeling at that moment, they can easily say "I'm hungry' rather than cry until you ask them if they want food.

Mood-charting can help a patient anticipate and identify their feelings at any point in time, so that they can avoid 'punishing' other people instead of looking inwards and tackling the issue from within them.

Mood-charting can be done with a pocket notebook, where the patient would have to record their moods and feelings at every hour of the day for a period of time, maybe a couple of weeks or months.

After some time, a pattern would emerge and it will be easy to tell how and what the patient may feel at different periods.

The patient would also be able to prepare themselves to handle the people and challenges that they are likely to come across during these periods.

- Family Therapy

The truth is that it is the family and friends that suffer most. If you are living with someone who suffers from BPD, it can take a negative toll on you and since the condition can be passed on to people who grew up or lived with BPD patients for a long time, your children may be at risk of developing Borderline Personality disorder too.

Family therapy is not only helpful for learning how to cope with, and live with patients without conflicts, it can also be a preventive or protective measure for people who have to live with or relate with a person who has the Borderline Personality Disorder.

Family therapy involves all members of the household working together with a therapist. You would all attend sessions as a group, where you would be taught how to communicate and cope with the patient, and how to avoid dangerous BPD family cycles from forming.

You would also be taught how to set boundaries and take care of yourself while caring for your loved one.

Family therapy is often more effective than individual therapy because the patient will still face difficulties at home if family and friends don't know how to communicate and live with them until their condition improves.

There are a lot of family therapy programs for Borderline Personality Disorder but a very common and effective one is Systems Training for Emotional Predictability and Problem-solving (STEPPS). It is a 20-week program that all family members have to attend. The program helps you learn how to predict the patient's reactions to common issues, and help you learn positive ways to respond, communicate and live with them.

Recovery Takes Time

Your loved one will get better as soon as they start receiving treatments but it is important to note that this will not happen overnight.

Some patients will get better almost immediately, while some might take years to respond to recovery so make sure you are patient with your loved one, and you give them as much time as they need to get better.

Chapter 7 Addressing and Changing Negative Behaviors and Patterns of BPD

The development tasks of the person concerned.

The success of the therapy therefore depends on the competence of the therapist, but also on the motivation of the person concerned and the quality of the relationship between the two.

A therapy can start at different points. It is obvious that the problems are updated in the therapy. Since the borderline disorder mainly affects the interpersonal area, the relationship between patient and therapist is the point at which the problems can be made clear. Updating the problems is certainly not enough, however, if solutions cannot also be found to get the symptoms and problems under control. These solutions usually require that the patient's strengths come to bear. Therapy therefore also serves to activate resources, especially in the search for alternative forms of life. In a certain sense, the therapy serves many affected persons not least to find a new meaning, i.e. to clarify the significance of the symptoms in life history. If the latter is successful, overcoming the disease can also result in maturation.

Specialized therapies differ less in the basic principles of therapy than in their orientation towards a specific disease model of the disorder. The mediation of this model thus represents a central element of specific therapy procedures. This enables a better concentration on the essential elements of the disease to be achieved, but the general factors of a disease to be given less consideration. Specific therapy methods are thus often embedded in a more general therapy plan.

Types of Therapy

In the history of therapy, a multitude of therapeutic methods have been developed. Essentially, however, biological, humanistic (including conversational psychotherapy, hypnotherapy, Gestalt therapy), psychoanalytic, cognitive-behavioral and systemic therapy methods are differentiated. Apart from a different understanding of illness, these therapeutic approaches differ primarily in their "therapeutic setting". This refers to the conditions under which the therapy takes place. Psychoanalysis works primarily with memory and free narration, cognitive behavior therapy with exercises and systemic therapy with the inclusion of the social environment, especially the family. The experiences with the different approaches and settings can vary greatly from patient to patient, so that it is not really possible to foresee which procedure the patient will benefit most from.

Therapeutic treatment will take place on an outpatient, day-care or inpatient basis. Inpatient treatment can take place in a responsible psychiatric clinic, but also in specialized facilities, such as certain psychosomatic hospitals. The decision as to which form of treatment is appropriate depends on the extent of the symptoms, the degree of risk and the need for help. However, other considerations are also important in deciding whether outpatient or inpatient treatment is more appropriate.

Outpatient therapy usually extends over a longer period of time, with the therapeutic contacts consisting of conversations between which there is usually an interval of at least one week. The advantage of outpatient therapy lies in the fact that contact with the social environment is maintained and the practice field of everyday life enables direct implementation of the therapy progress. In the case of inpatient treatment, the therapeutic programmed is more extensive and thus the therapeutic contact is closer. Instead, there is no opportunity to practice in everyday life. In addition, an inpatient stay involves confrontation with other patients. This can have advantages and disadvantages. However, in the context of an inpatient stay, the distance from the demands of everyday life often makes a beneficial distance and relief possible, so that forces for change can be released.

Some may be admitted to an acute ward of a psychiatric hospital as part of a crisis intervention. Occasionally such an emergency admission represents the beginning of a more intensive therapeutic correction of the disorder. However, psychiatric wards are rarely able to provide specific treatment. However, even treatment wards in psychiatric hospitals are not always geared to the therapy of personality disorders. In such treatment wards one is of course also confronted with patients suffering from other mental illnesses. This can have advantages and disadvantages. In specialised wards, the therapy programmed is usually adapted to the disorder and the group of patients is more homogeneous. However, waiting times and long journeys often have to be accepted.

With all alternatives, it is always advantageous to obtain information beforehand when selecting a suitable setting, so that the special features of the individual options can be carefully weighed against each other.

Expectations of the Therapy

"Even if I am diagnosed with this disorder, I am still the same person and do not intend to see myself as a 'carrier of a disease with certain symptoms', but as a person with personal traits. I will not hide behind a certificate. In general, my fellow human beings either get along very well with me spontaneously or I spontaneously cause allergic reactions, one of them, there is no middle."

In contrast to other mental disorders, it is not to be expected that all aspects of a borderline disorder can be treated and changed during therapy. At the beginning of a therapy there is often the need to do something or the urge of others that something must happen. Expectations therefore often fluctuate between "everything or nothing". But both are unrealistic.

In general, therapy cannot bring about an immediate change in the way we live our lives, but serves to expand the patient's ability to cope with the symptoms caused by the disease. Therapy is therefore a kind of empowerment. The transfer of experiences within the therapy to the handling of symptoms and the general shaping of life is a service that the patient has to provide above all. This transfer will be particularly successful if the expectations and the goals developed from them are as concrete as possible. This is the only way to find a benchmark for the development and success of a therapy. The following questions and answers clearly reflect these expectations and experiences with inpatient therapy.

Changing symptoms and coping with them

What conditions and prerequisites are necessary for therapy to benefit you?

Confidence that you feel well and that you can be helped.

Enlightenment. The therapist should be trained and sometimes rebuke me.

I would have to be halfway balanced, so that I am really receptive. I should be able to develop trust, feel understood and accepted. In the time of the therapy I should be exposed to as little stress as possible from outside (family, friends, colleagues etc.), so that I can stay in the here and now.

Conversations, therapy and that one understands oneself here with the people. That I also see and cooperate.

The important thing is the attitude and the insight to the therapy. To want to give and to get involved in changes. In addition a minimum of confidence belongs to it. Then courage is also needed to let new things in. And the insight that I did not get along with the previous patterns. In addition, learning to accept change.

Confidence to the therapist, best a protected framework.

Structure, clarity, regularity, truth, everything may say, about me speak, sympathy.

Which therapeutic measures do you find helpful?

I like skill trainings, sports and individual conversations.

My experience is that both music therapy and body awareness, social competence training, individual discussions with the therapist and nursing staff, conversations with those affected, the beautiful park for extended walks, all these measures have contributed to strengthening.

Social competence training, skill training, sports, employment, therapy, fitness and the self-help group help me.

At that time I did not want to come here and I went on strike against it because I believed that I did not need therapy and that nobody could help me because nobody understood me. That is why I attempted suicide. Later, training might also be based on the fact that I was here so long and could learn so much.

The most important thing for me is skill training. This is how I learn most about myself, my way of thinking, my mistakes and my behavior. This is the best prerequisite for tackling change.

Both working on current difficulties and getting to know each other better as well as working with dreams.

To be able to talk about everything, a well-reflected therapist who knows when I am lost or when I want to mislead him, i.e. someone who knows his soul and has a map and knows where what lies and how to get there.

How can you help yourself?

By using the skills, I try to calm down or lower myself, otherwise I try to talk to someone. Sometimes I listen to music, try to sleep or talk on the phone.

With the emergency skill training kit. What I learned in the conversations, to use the skills regularly and to try out almost everything that will suggest.

By collaborating and paying close attention to myself, that I can cope later.

I help myself in various ways. Once about the confrontation with myself. I find out what does me good and what the next steps are to implement it. Then I keep a diary in which my feelings get space. I take daily walks. I provide variety. I look at everything from different angles and draw conclusions for today. I create positive ideas about the future and ask myself what I need for it.

Which topics bring you closer to your goal of becoming healthy?

How best to cope with the disease, for example what you can do in case of a crisis.

Topics that concern everyday life and the various areas of life, such as partnership, social environment, workplace, leisure activities, family and friendships.

The most important thing for me is the past, which I would have to deal with.

What information will help you better understand your condition?

How to calm down better. How to get rid of anger without hurting anyone and breaking objects.

Anything that helps to analyze the disease.

Experiences of others in similar situations to mine.

Information that I would otherwise not be able to access, which is very much in the medical field. Information, which refers to empirical values.

What significance does your family have in participating in the therapy?

It has the meaning that everyone can see what the experience is like for me. The acceptance of being able to leave something behind, to find new possibilities for an independent life of one's own.

I am dependent on the support of the family, the understanding and their patience, if not everything is to break.

How do you know you're feeling better?

I can tell by how I manage to fulfill my life's desires and cope better with S. and also have a lot of understanding for her.

I am calm, feel well, no tension, positive thoughts, feelings, future plans, can be more patient.

I scratch much less, have a normal weight and only very rarely suicidal thoughts and tensions.

On my sleeping behavior, when I live in the here and now, when I feel the joy of life, when I can make plans again, when I get out of bed well in the morning.

Therapy is always a process in which goals and expectations change continuously. In the best case, the developments within the framework of therapy open up new avenues. The solution through therapy is often the fact that the spectrum of possibilities expands.

Reasons for a Therapy

As a rule, the thought of a therapy comes when the pressure of suffering has become so great that one can no longer progress with one's own means. The advice of friends, perhaps also occasionally coincidences, then consolidate the intention. Of course, the therapy should relieve the strain of suffering and reduce the symptoms. It should be remembered that no real success is conceivable without an inner change. Therapy does not only mean that something changes, but also that the affected person is ready for a change and can also carry out this change. Some people literally flee into therapy because they can no longer bear the pressure of the disease.

This motive is initially legitimate, after all therapy is also a shelter. But the shelter must be left strengthened, because the demands of life still have to be met. Therapy is also not an end in itself. It can only be a component of the personal life organization and life accomplishment. This spectrum becomes clear in the following report:

I decided to save my life after I "made myself go away" every day with brutally a lot of alcohol. My best and only friend was alcohol and my biggest enemy was myself. The first thing I did was to detoxify myself and I received a lot of positive support. To protect myself I stayed there for two months (the rule is two weeks). I then decided to go to a day clinic because I still thought I was strong enough to cope with life and therapy at the same time. The day clinic was not worth the name. So I started to organize a long-term therapy for myself. I didn't get any support from the clinic side, so I did everything on my own (pride). Then I had different clinics send me therapy concepts (not these cute house brochures) and decided afterwards.

Therapy concept: deep psychological orientation. Forms of therapy: Art, sport, Gestalt, group and individual therapy. The concept points out that borderlines are increasingly to be found among the patients and that the clinic is not necessarily able to do justice to them. I found that honest.

Conclusion: I went into therapy with a sense of self-esteem that I was under the turf and went out with my shoulders over the grass. I pulled the best out of every single form of therapy for myself (I can't believe it, but you can learn to even get rid of your anger in the artistic field - I didn't even count the brushes afterwards). Otherwise, I have learned to perceive feelings and to endure them, to better differentiate myself. In short, I got to know myself better.

Afterwards I did a follow-up therapy, which consisted of individual and group therapy and was excellent. My individual therapist has never been obsessed with the subject of addiction, but has dealt with the subject of borderline.

In conclusion, I can only say that there is no "wrong" or "right" therapy. A therapy can only bring as much benefit as one is willing to contribute. The prerequisite for this is, on the one hand, surrendering to oneself and, on the other hand, the willingness to endure the consequences of a therapy.

I cannot say that my life today has become simpler, but at least more understandable, and I know today how and where I can find help when life is no longer bearable.

Experiences with Therapists

The experiences with therapists are quite different. Thus, bad experiences do not mean that a therapy cannot be used. It is not easy to define the suitability of a therapist. Experience certainly plays a major role, but the therapist's attitude towards the affected person and his attitude towards the disorder also have an influence on the quality of the therapeutic contact. The therapy of the borderline disorder was also burdened for a long time by the fact that violent conflicts were expected from the therapist in advance. Nevertheless, the patient also bears responsibility for the success of the therapeutic relationship.

All those who have dealt with the treatment of borderline disorders emphasize the importance of the "container" function in therapy. This refers to the therapist's ability to absorb and endure the patient's emotions - the "supporting" function of the therapy. An important prerequisite for this is that a therapist is able to cope with crises of the

and patients can deal with. It is also necessary to strike a balance between closeness and distance. If a therapist behaves distantly and prefers critical comments, it is very difficult to achieve sufficient openness in the therapeutic relationship. On the other hand, being too close to the problems makes sober reflection more difficult and increases the risk of uncontrolled reactions. In this sense, it is always an advantage if the therapist can also question himself and consider his own limitations.

It has already been mentioned above that the person concerned can also contribute to a good therapeutic relationship. For example, a certain reliability in keeping agreements is important. Refusal to cooperate, for example due to a lack of openness, can also put a lasting strain on the therapeutic relationship. This includes concealing additional alcohol and drug consumption.

Many of the symptoms associated with the disorder may overburden therapists. Considering the limitations of a therapist is a protection against the failure of the therapy. It is important that the private area remains protected. Even enduring threats has its limits. For example, frequent announcements of suicidal actions are a permanent threat to therapy. Due to the relationship disorder within the framework of the borderline disorder, those affected tend to adopt a "hostile" attitude towards the therapist. It is not to be expected that a therapist can directly offer a solution to all situations. Impatience will therefore negatively affect the therapist's motivation to comment on the person's stories. A therapeutic relationship in which mutual reproaches and devaluations occur in the first place cannot succeed in the long run.

There are many behaviors on the part of the therapist that play a role in therapeutic relationships. The necessary distance has already been mentioned above. It cannot be helpful for a therapist to be anxious to make the patient dependent on himself. Such a danger is particularly present when a therapist overestimates his own possibilities. But also a strong uncertainty as well as the disregard of one's own emotions can have a negative influence on the course of the therapy. It is actually necessary for a therapist to establish a balance between acceptance and willingness to change. Such a balance becomes particularly clear in the above example.

It is important for a therapist to insist on adherence to rules while maintaining flexibility. The therapist's openness is also important, because it is usually of great interest to the person concerned what a therapist thinks. If mutual openness is achieved, critical remarks can also be better accepted.

Finding the right Therapist

"My first therapy was after a suicide attempt. My therapist at that time asked me (I was abused by my own father) as nice questions as I did: What did you do to irritate your father? Or: Could you imagine sleeping with me? Nevertheless, I risked trusting a therapist again and didn't regret it."

It is always difficult to find the right therapy and the right therapist for the diversity of the offer. As a rule, the possibilities of information are also limited. It is advantageous if the experiences of other patients can be used. However, this is only possible in exceptional cases. Perhaps the situation will improve with the introduction of the Internet. At first, however, one is usually dependent on the principle of trial and error. At the beginning of this search there should be a consultation. The consultation can take place from a professional, in addition, from friends and possibly from co-affected ones. Occasionally it is no mistake to consult a doctor with this question. It is also possible to seek advice from a psychiatrist or information from outpatient psychotherapists. In many places there are also counselling centers that can help in the search for a suitable therapist. Sometimes health insurance companies have information at their disposal.

Psychotherapy is the primary treatment for borderline disorders. It can therefore be carried out by an appropriately trained doctor or psychological psychotherapist. It has already been mentioned above that the inpatient services are also specialized in different ways. As a rule, the individual clinics have information material from which the degree of specialization can be seen.

The addresses of outpatient therapists can be obtained from the telephone directory, better still from the health insurance company or within the framework of the above-mentioned consultations. Since in many cases an outpatient treatment is carried out first, it is possible to ask for the addresses of the clinics in question. If possible, an initial consultation should be arranged before starting the therapy. The treatment conditions can be clarified and a first impression can be gained about the way of dealing with the disorder. For example, in the case of additional alcohol and drug abuse, an upstream detoxification treatment is sometimes required.

It is not only important to find the right therapist, but also to correct wrong decisions. In this sense, it is a good idea to reflect together with the therapist on the course of treatment at certain intervals and to evaluate it with regard to expectations. If there is no noticeable progress, a break in treatment or a change in therapy can possibly be agreed.

Chapter 8 Reconstructing Your World and Building a New You

Talking treatment, psychological therapy and talking therapy all mean the same thing. These terms have the same meaning and all cover treatments that you may know as: • Psychotherapy • Counseling • Therapy Some will use one of the terms while others will use another term. This can be confusing, but they are all talking about the same thing. Specially trained mental health professionals practice therapy. A therapist can also be referred to as a psychiatrist, psychologist, psychotherapist and counselor What Talking Treatments Can Help You With

You open your mouth to talk to your counselor and words just tumble out of your mouth. That's okay, because your therapist will still likely make sense of it all, and translate it back so it even makes sense to you.

Talking treatments can help you deal with difficult feelings or experiences you are going through like: • Bereavement • Anger • Fear • Guilt • Low self-esteem • Redundancy • Sadness • A relationship breakup • Anxiety • Depression Talking treatments can help you to cope and to come to terms with the symptoms you experience, along with your mental distress, illness, disability or physical problems.

Cognitive Behavior Therapy or CBT

Cognitive Behavioral Therapy helps you tackle day-to-day difficulties using problem-solving techniques. You will learn how you can replace negative thinking patterns with positive ones.

Cognitive Behavioral Therapy generally focuses on the present, but when used for BPD, it also takes into account your past experiences, which have had an influence on your current fundamental beliefs and how you think.

Problem-Solving Therapy (PST)

Problem Solving Therapy is a talking therapy that is based on the use of cognitive-behavioral techniques. It is helpful if you are depressed or if you are in a crisis after an attempt to commit suicide. The focus of Problem Solving Therapy is the present and there are five stages: • Adopt a problem-solving strategy • Define the problem and select your goals • Think of potential solutions • Predict possible results and choose the solution that is best • Try it and look at the effects Generally, there are four to eight sessions for PST. During these sessions your therapist and will work with you to identify the problems you are facing, and then you will focus on one or more of the problems while your therapist teaches you a structured approach to help you solve your problems. Your therapist will also teach you a general approach to your problems.

Your therapist will decide whether to use PST as a complete structure for your therapy sessions or to use PST with other therapies.

Problem Solving Therapy is a series of seven steps, which we will look at.

1. Problem Orientation

This is your attitude to solve issues and problems. This is not your actual problem solving skills, but rather it relates to your thoughts and feelings about the problem(s) and your ability to solve the problem(s). These two components determine how you are going to respond when you face a stressful problem. That's why it is such a key part of your PST.

Positive problem orientation is associated with an effective, rational style of solving problems while negative problem solving is associated with a problem solving style that is one of avoidance. You are likely to make careless, impulsive decisions. One of the main goals of PST is to help you develop positive orientation through education and helping you to recognize when your attitude is negative.

2. Recognize and Identify Problems

Step 2 aims to teach you how you can recognize a problem, identify the problem correctly and begin to solve it. While it sounds pretty obvious written down, it is not always that straightforward, because you are accustomed to avoiding your problems or impulsively responding.

There are three parts to Step 2:

• Invite you to impulsively report current problems • Learn how to track problem indicators • Using a problem checklist

3. Select and Define a Clear Problem

The third step in problem solving therapy helps you to choose one clear problem to work on and define. Learning how to define a problem clearly is important because the more clearly you can define a problem the easier solutions will be to find. Fuzzy problems get fuzzy solutions. You can achieve clear definition by gathering all the facts and then clearly and objectively writing them down.

4. Generate Solutions

Once you have selected and defined the problem you are going to work on, you will need to begin problem solving to identify possible solutions. You will learn how to brainstorm. The more ideas you have, the more you are likely to find a solution that will work.

5. Decision Making

Once you identify some possible solutions, you need to make a decision by weighing the advantages and disadvantages of each potential solution. You might find this stage difficult because there are so many possible solutions going around in your mind. Your therapist will teach you a systematic way to make these decisions.

The Hidden Signs of Borderline Personality Disorder

While many of the symptoms of borderline personality disorder are difficult to miss, there are also traits of the illness that are much more subtle. A person exhibiting these more subtle signs is said to be experiencing "quiet" borderline personality disorder.

Whereas people with BPD often experience violent mood swings which are easy to recognise, those with quiet BPD are more likely to internalize their feelings. While they still experience the same fluctuation of emotions, the disorder can be much more difficult to spot.

To recognize "quiet" BPD in either yourself or a loved one, look out for the following traits and symptoms:

- Struggling to maintain relationships: People with quiet BPD may speak about how they find it hard to keep relationships, whether romantic or otherwise. These relationships will often have been ended by the other person, unable to cope with the BPD sufferer's wild mood swings and aggression.

- Low self-esteem: While quiet sufferers of BPD may be less prone to self-damaging behavior such as reckless driving or violence, they are still likely to suffer from a severely diminished sense of self-worth. Often, this will only be noticeable to others by paying attention to the way they speak about themselves. They may say things like "I can't do anything right," or "Why would you want to spend time with me?"

- Self-harming tendencies and talk of suicide: As with the above example, to recognize these traits in quiet sufferers of BPD, it is important to pay attention to the way they speak. Their comments relating to self-harm or suicide might seem on the surface to be flippant, throw-away lines such as "It makes me want to bash my head against a brick wall," or but this seemingly innocuous comments can be a mask for much deeper issues.

- Having Unhealthy Boundaries: In the same way that BPD sufferers are prone to black and white thinking, people with quiet BPD will often obsess about a person, seeming to care greatly what this person thinks of them. On the flip side, they may also have times of needing to completely detach from others, pulling away to the point of isolating themselves in order to create what they perceive as a safe space between them and the world.

- Heightened Emotions: People suffering from BPD generally experience emotions much more easily and deeply than the general population. This can have both negative and positive effects. People with BPD often exhibit great levels of excitement, enthusiasm, joy and love but, conversely, can often feel overwhelmed by negative emotions such as anxiety, depression, guilt, anger. Everyday emotions are often highlighted, with sadness being transmuted to grief, for example, mild embarrassment being replaced by intense humiliation and panic taking the place of nervousness.

- Lack of concentration: Another more subtle trait of BPD is the inability to concentrate. This is often due to the intense emotions building up inside one's head, leaving them with little room to think about anything else. Inability to concentrate is a form of disassociation and can appear as though a person is simply zoning out. A BPD sufferer who has zoned out can be identified by an expressionless face and/or flat vocal delivery. They may also appear distracted.

Familiarizing yourself with these more subtle symptoms of borderline personality disorder can help you identify whether you or a loved one may be suffering from the illness. If you suspect yourself or someone you love is experience borderline personality disorder, it is important to seek professional help.

The Different Faces of Borderline Personality Disorder - Types of BPD

J Borderline personality disorder can also be broken down into four different types, as proposed by American psychologist Theodore Million, in his 1995 book Disorders of Personality DSM-IV and Beyond.

Million's four categories of BPD are as follows:

- Discouraged Borderline: People suffering from discouraged borderline personalities often exhibit avoidant, depressive, dependent tendencies. People with this form of BPD are often submissive and humble, and prone to pliant behavior. They often feel hopeless, powerless and vulnerable. Someone with a discouraged borderline personality can be clingy and tends to go along with the crowd for fear of upsetting the people around them. They can behave in a somber and dejected manner. Below the surface, however, is an anger waiting to erupt. When it does so, it can lead sufferers to self-injury and even suicide.

- Petulant Borderline: A petulant borderline personality is characterized by a heightened sense of negativity. Sufferers of this form of BPD are often highly impatient, stubborn and resentful. They are sullen and defiant and feel easily slighted. They are easily disillusion and disappointed in life. People with a petulant borderline personality disorder fluctuate between desperately relying on people and keeping their distance out of fear of being disappointed or let down. Their emotions are prone to swing between feelings of unworthiness and rage.

- Impulsive borderline: Sufferers of impulsive borderline personalities are prone to histrionic or antisocial behavior. This form of BPD is characterized by frenetic, flighty behavior. They can often be flirty and charismatic, able to draw people to them. They are highly energetic and are constantly seeking the next thrill. However, when things do not go their way, sufferers are quick to become agitated, gloomy and irritable. They fear any form of loss, leading them to frequent suicidal tendencies.

- Self-destructive borderline: Self-destructive borderline personalities are often highly depressive and masochistic. They carry around a constant sense of bitterness, which they regularly turn inwards. People with this form of BPD are often prone to self-harming and self-punishing. They are often angry, highly strung and moody and are prone to suicidal thoughts and behaviors. Their self-hatred is prone to reach extreme levels, leading them to many types of destructive behavior, ranging from reckless driving, to poor healthcare, to performing derogatory sexual acts.

In addition to these four borderline types proposed by Million, psychologist Dr. Christine Lawson also identified four types of borderline personalities in her book Understanding the Borderline Mother.

- Borderline Queen: Someone with a borderline queen personality is prone to perfectionism. They are prone to take mild criticism very personally and will become aggressive and indignant if anyone suggests they have made a mistake. Thanks to their perfectionism, borderline queens often disassociate from their own negative traits and emotions, believing them a flaw, so is often unable to accept his or her own mistakes. People with this borderline personality regularly feel the need to one-up people around them, particularly their therapists and loved ones.

- Borderline Waif: Unlike many other borderline types, the borderline waif does not exhibit a great deal of aggression or outward hostility. Instead, they appear to be fragile and victimized by all life has thrown at them. Waifs are generally depressed and discontented and worry easily. Borderline waifs believe themselves to be helpless victims and often refuse to accept help in order to keep their 'victim' mentality alive.

- Borderline Witch: Someone exhibiting a borderline witch personality can be extremely aggressive and controlling. They seek to punish people for the smallest of indiscretions and are prone to "borderline rage" -- the destruction of objects that are of value to those they believe have wronged them. Borderline witches are adept at black and white thinking, particularly when it comes to their loved ones. Parents with this personality will often idealize one of their children over the rest or seek to play one family member off against another. People with a borderline witch personality can be extremely domineering and intrusive, often violating the boundaries of those around them. They are prone to using the thoughts and feelings of those around them a weapon, leading their loved ones to become withdrawn and restrained in their presence. Borderline witches can be extremely paranoid and suspicious, with their hostile behavior masking their own fear of loss of control.

- Borderline Hermit: People with a borderline hermit personality view the world as an inherently dangerous place. They have large amounts of paranoia and suspicion and have trouble trusting those around them. Thanks to their belief that everyone is out to get them, borderline hermits will withdraw from the world and isolate themselves. For many sufferers of a borderline hermit personality, the disorder stems from sexual abuse or other equally damaging childhood trauma.

Diagnosing Borderline Personality Disorder

A BPD can lead to violence, damaged relationships, any number of dangerous behaviors, and even suicide. It is not something that you should attempt to handle without the help of a trained psychologist, or other mental health professional.

Self Diagnoses:

- Do your emotions change very quickly?

- Do you often experience extreme anger, sadness or distress?

- Do you often feel empty or unfulfilled?

- Are you constantly afraid the people I care about with leave me?

- Are most of your romantic relationships intense and unstable?

- Does the way you feel about the people in your life tend to fluctuate from one extreme to the other?

- Are you ever tempted to engage in self-injury or attempt suicide?

- When you feel insecure in a relationship, do you ever lash out or behave impulsively in a desperate attempt to keep your lover close?

- Do you ever engage in dangerous behavior such as binge drinking, drug use, unsafe sex or reckless driving?

If you or your loved one answered yes to several or all of these statements, it may indicate borderline personality disorder.

Professional Diagnoses:

BPD will be officially diagnosed following a clinical assessment by a mental health professional. The generally accepted method of diagnosis involves presenting the patient with a list of characteristics and asking them whether they feel such characteristics accurately represents them. By actively involving patients in their own diagnosis this way, sufferers are likely to come to terms with the disorder more quickly.

Mental health experts have produced a list of nine symptoms associated with borderline personality disorder. For a person to be diagnosed with BPD, they must exhibit at least five of the following traits:

- Fear of abandonment

- Unclear or changing self-image

- Unstable relationships

- Impulsive and/or self-destructive behaviors

- Tendency towards self-hard or suicide attempts

- Extreme mood swings

- Difficulty controlling rage

- Paranoia or suspicion of others' motives.

- Persistent feelings of emptiness

Such an evaluation will also discuss the severity of these symptoms and when they began, along with determining when they may have begun. Of particular relevance are any suicidal thoughts a patient may have experienced, along with thoughts of self-harm, or doing harm to others.

An assessment may also include physical tests to rule out other triggers of these symptoms, such as thyroid conditions or drug and alcohol abuse.

As a result, mental health professionals might experiment with a range of treatments and therapies in order to identify the most suitable path towards recovery.

So what if you or a loved one has been diagnosed with borderline personality disorder? What does this mean for your relationships, and your life in general? There is no doubt that

BPD presents an enormous array of challenges to both the sufferer and those around them. But all is not lost.

What to Expect if You Have Been Diagnosed with Borderline Personality Disorder

So you have been diagnosed with borderline personality disorder. Perhaps this has come as a cruel shock. Or perhaps you may even welcome the diagnosis as an explanation to your previously unexplainable emotional outbursts and mood swings. It feel like a relief to know that this behavior is the cause of an illness, rather than another part of yourself.

Regardless of how you feel about your diagnosis, there is no doubt that living with borderline personality disorder can be a hellish experience, both for you and your loved ones. BPD can affect every part of your life, from your relationship to yourself and others, to your education, career and recreational life. Your tendencies to act out and behave in violent and aggressive mean that both you and your loved ones are prone to being hurt, both physically and mentally.

Learning to manage the disorder begins with understand. By knowing exactly what to expect, you can prepare and develop coping skills to help you weather the emotional storm. Having a deep understanding of your illness and its traits will also help you communicate better with your loved ones about BPD, making it easier for them to assist you with the struggles you will face.

Chapter 9 Maintain success on a personal level

The most important part of an abusive relationship might be the first moment within it—the first contact you make with your abuser. This first contact you make may be the most important part of that relationship. The way that we make first contact with a person and the way that an abuser makes first contact with a person are massively different, and this shows most of all when we first meet them. That first stage of that relationship is led by that first touch, the first impressions of both parties.

As a victim, when we meet someone, we think about what they're thinking and what that might lead to. As people who have a tendency to live in fear and anxiety for most of our lives after being in the cycle of abuse, we look for a way to escape from almost everywhere we find ourselves. When we're trained as people to be afraid of our partners, we don't have the positive experiences with other people, which would assure us to act more calmly.

However, we look at new people we meet as just that—as normal people, more or less. Normal people grow up meeting new people by spending time around them and checking for themselves if they get a good feeling from that person. This is how we're used to interacting with people, and we treat most other people we meet like non-threatening presences. We understand the world around us as relatively safe and we connect with people out of a desire for security and companionship. We check if their "vibe" is one that we connect with.

Most normal people have a sense of character and are able to read people for their true characters easily. Some people are a better judge of character than others, but most normal people have in common that they spend their time understanding someone better simply through practice. Spending time with someone you know better is the fastest way to get to know them on a more personal level. It's through this repeated interaction that we become closer to other people. That interaction forges a new relationship with them over time, and we get to know them even better. This is the cycle for most normal people, socially.

Abusers, on the other hand, very rarely act this way when they first meet someone. When an abuser first meets someone, they try to sniff out the weaknesses of other people. They look at a person as someone who could act as a steppingstone or another pawn for them to get where they think they need to go. They use everyone they meet is they think there's something in it for them, and that mainly includes potential victims for a relationship. When you first meet them, they'll analyze you to try to find out how you function. Abusers usually have a lack of understanding of how people function, so they're mainly focused on understanding people they meet on the most literal level.

This is where abusers locate empaths, in particular—highly sensitive people are usually able to be picked out of a crowd, especially by manipulative people and abusers. Empaths are usually very reactive to meeting new people and will show their emotions on their faces very plainly. They react expressively to the feelings of other people, and the abuser understands this and uses it to their advantage by trying to draw emotional responses out of them. When they do so, the confirm to themselves that they're meeting someone very empathetic, likely to try to sympathize with them whenever they can. In addition, the abuser will try to see if they can gauge how submissive you are when the two of you first meet.

As you spend more time with them, they will offer you more opportunities to defer to them and let them do what they want instead of offering you that opportunity. The more you allow them to exert their will over you at these opportunities, the more the abuser is assured that they can do so farther into the relationship. This entire set of first meetings between the abuser and their victim is the set-up for abuse. They groom their victims, trying to scope out what part of their personality they can take advantage of and to what degree.

When they come into contact with a new person, they immediately begin to look at that person as either someone expendable to their grand plan or someone who they need to keep around for at least the time being. Those who he does keep around are the victims who are often the most empathetic, the most kind to them, the most willing and able to see the good in people and the good in bad people, in particular. Seeing this potential for good things in all people, no matter their past actions, is good and kind.

However, not being able to balance this kind lens with a sense of realism and what the person is likely to do of their own volition, can end with you getting hurt by that person. The same person who you may have thought you could save at one point, could end up being your undoing, your new abuser. They can turn out to be someone who manipulates and uses you for a large portion of your life in the future, a portion of your life that's incredibly hard to fight your way out of. Being able to just look at everyone you meet more sensibly can be your answer. Dodging the potential for meeting a terrible and manipulative person by developing your ability to be cautious around new people, instead of either blindly latching onto them or blindly avoiding them. Picking and choosing who you associate, instead, can be a much more positive solution.

After you make that first important contact with your abuser, and they decide you're someone they want to keep around for their own sake, they'll initiate the second phase of their plan. This phase is often referred to as "love-bombing," the infamous phase in which the abuser showers their victims with affection and praise and essentially induces a high in the victim.

When we first enter a relationship, we enter the honeymooning phase of that relationship, in which we experience elation pretty much every time we're around that person. Our new partner is put on a pedestal in our eyes, and we can't stop thinking about them. We romanticize just about everything they do, right down to the way they move and breathe. This first infatuation phase happens because the new partner and a new relationship introduce a lot of dopamine into our system.

This dopamine, a neurotransmitter often associated with rewards and risk-taking, floods our brains when we think about or interact with that new partner. This is what infatuation is, chemically speaking. The dopamine floods the brain over and over again and this heightened level of the chemical leads to extended and heightened feelings of giddiness, joy, elation, and excitement. This is the feeling of falling in love when we first meet our partner and enter a serious relationship with them. That feeling can last a long time, and the abusive partner knows how to take advantage of it. When we're right in the middle of this honeymooning phase, the abuser will love-bomb us by showing us lots of tender affection.

In a way, this softer version of their normal beginning praise and attention offsets the dopamine flooding our brain, but the abuser is also keen on how most abuse victims think and react. Large, over the top shows of love can be frightening at first, especially to someone who's afraid of attachment or being left behind, so the abuser pulls back.

Instead of these massive shows of love or infatuation on their end, they introduce the victim to flowers, handholding, gentle and soft ways, they show affection and love. In addition to this softer side of the new partner, they know how to make the abuse victim feel special as well. They'll introduce parts of themselves that are vulnerable, even secret, assuring the partner that they've never told anyone else these things about themselves. They pretend to bare their heart and soul to their partner, in an attempt to get their trust almost immediately—and it usually works.

While this act of vulnerability usually earns the trust of their newest victim, it also ensnares them into thinking that their new partner can be saved, helped, turned around down the road when the relationship begins to turn sour. When the abuser starts to act out, the victim is under the impression that they do these things and act sourly because of the damage they might have endured when they were younger. The abuser sets the precedent when the relationship is still good and pleasant, revealing some damaging truth to you beforehand. It helps them to garner sympathy from you. You want to help them and try to heal them as best you can, especially if you're someone who considers yourself an empath. This is the other reason most abusers will try to pick out an empath as their newest partner and victim—an empath is most likely to connect to them and their story, whichever story that is. When the abuser presents themselves as something like a victim of abuse in their younger years, they develop a kinship with their victim. The victim will usually reciprocate the feeling, as they're usually trying to forge some kind of bond with the people they meet anyway.

Someone who has probably been abused before is going to try their hardest to connect to people who have also endured abuse before. Therefore, the abuser has the means and the ability to forcibly connect themselves and their feelings to those of their partner, who is likely an empath—someone who feels a heightened connection to the emotions of others. After that connection is made, it's hard for the victim to separate from the other side of the connection on their own. The abuser has made room for themselves to act out and begin abusing and more brashly manipulating their victims. They feel more able to now, as they've established themselves as someone who can connect with their partner on a deeper level than most other people.

After that precedent is established along with their connection through trauma, the victim is compelled to give them more chances, to offer them more help. They're convinced that their abuser is simply misguided, just misdirected and in need of help. They're more than willing to outstretch their hand, feeling the pain of their partner, and try to give their partner help. The victim, like I've said before, can develop a bit of a hero complex—they believe that because they weren't able to receive the help they wanted when they needed it, they can be the saving grace of other people who are being abused or going through a hard time.

Ultimately, the abuser will use this optimism against the partner, which will keep the victim of their abuse closer to them as time goes on. The more strongly the victim believes they can save their partner, the less likely it is that the victim will be able to leave of their own volition. To them, if they leave their abuser behind, they'll be giving up on them and the cause they had been dedicating themselves to. In reality, this is exactly what the abuser wants out of their victim—any reason for them to want to stick around and be helpful to the abuser. The more the victim is willing to help, the more subservient they tend to be when the victim plays them right.

The next phase might come as a surprise to most victims who are coming right out of the honeymooning phase of their new relationship. The part of the abusive relationship that follows this phase full of praise and love-bombing is the exact opposite—the devaluation phase. This is the sadder part of the relationship where the partner starts to draw back all of that praise and excitement, they had given you for so long. They start to replace the praise and the intimacy you had with them with strict rules and backhanded compliments to break you down and make you feel worthless.

In normal, healthy relationships, what comes after the honeymooning phase is the opposite of that rush of dopamine. The feel-good chemical which had been flooding the brain for months, even years, dries up back to a relatively normal level.

Because dopamine, along with most other neurotransmitters, can be chemically addictive, we get used to that rush of dopamine that we had when we began the relationship. We want to ride that high forever, and so the crash afterward is just that much harder. The emotional low after the honeymooning period is where most relatively short-term relationships will come to an end because the two people will start to want to be around one another less and less as time goes on.

As they have this falling out, they get into fights more often and generally feel less and less in tune with each other. The high of infatuation and the elation of wanting your happy ending fades and you're faced with a flawed human in front of you. This revelation is jarring to people, and they usually can't help but feel more than a little disappointed. Hence, the two separate and see other people, for the cycle of elation and disappointment to perhaps repeat. The emotional low in a normal relationship is healthy—it's just the hormones in the human brain going back to a normal level.

Although it can feel as though you're drained, waiting out the emotional low will allow your brain to adjust to the new level of dopamine and other neurotransmitters. Your emotional responses to the person will also become calmer and more moderate. Your connection with that person becomes less infatuation and more actual intimate human connection—this is where "true" love actually begins.

In an abusive relationship, however, that infatuation was manipulated by the abuser to make the victim think that their elation was how the relationship should always be. That level of elevated happiness and elevated reaction, in general, is set as the standard for the two people by the manipulative partner. Then, after that connection is built and the victim is made to feel responsible for the abuser, the abuser takes back the kind things they had done for them. The intimacy and the vulnerability that the two had shared is erased, and a lot of changes happen between the two people. Where there was once kind, gentle gestures of love, the abuser now shows their "caring" nature by setting rules and restricting the victim. They withdraw their affection from you, make you feel like less of a person. The frequent texts and charming surprises slow or halt entirely, and their interactions with you might become colder, more isolated. They give you the cold shoulder, ignore you and your efforts, and treat you more like an inconvenience than a partner.

That connection you might have felt you shared through trauma or through the issues the two of you shared may feel like it's vanishing. In the place of that vulnerability, the abuser suddenly has this massive cold wall between you and them. They seem distant and like they don't want to do much with you, like go out or have dinner. The cute moments you had with them where you really clicked stop. They might even make it seem as though they feel sad, alone, frustrated, angry about something. They close themselves off from you and from other people, and you feel pressured to do the same for their sake. This is where the victim falls for the abuser's ultimate trap, one that's been laid out since the beginning of the relationship.

Because the victim already feels as though they and their abuser are connected through trauma, hardship, or something else intimate that the abuser revealed to their victim, they also feel like they have to suffer with the abuser. They think that they should sacrifice their social life or their happiness because it seems that their partner is being forced to do the same.

Because they feel like the intimate connection from before has been lost, they also feel that they have a responsibility to rekindle that relationship now with some other form of camaraderie. Alternately, the victim might feel like this colder version of their partner has been created by something the victim did. They might feel like they've been doing something wrong, not listening well enough to their partner or not doing something expected of them. They want to right that wrong, and so the victim doubles their efforts to help their partner, further investing themselves in that relationship, even though it's tearing them apart from the inside.

This hero complex that the victim has, and which has been developing with their partner for some time really comes into effect now as they do everything they can to please their abusers. When their partner seems upset or is ignoring them, the victim feels responsible for that. They feel like everything bad that happens to the both of them is somehow their fault—and the abuser knows this. They're aware of the effect they're having on their victim because they've had it intentionally set up that way since they first began interacting with each other.

From the moment the two people met, the abuser knew exactly how to ruin the positive feelings of their victim and how to get rid of them with little to no mess for them to clean up afterward.

That mess is also known as the discard phase. This is the part that hurts the most for the victim, as they may finally realize that the relationship and the connection, they had been building up inside their head doesn't actually exist. The love and responsibility they felt over caring for, protecting their partner, wasn't reciprocated. This is where the damage is done in the long term to the victim of the abuser, as they reel and have to take in that they weren't cared about at all during their relationship after all. Coming to terms with the fact that your relationship was actually hollow and wasn't filled with the love and compassion that you have thought was inside it, is incredibly hurtful for the victim in question.

After that realization on the part of the victim, they'll often get caught in the cycle of abuse where they want to leave and know that they should. But they keep getting drawn back in over and over again until they either find the courage to leave for good, or the abuser simply discards them for their next victim. As a victim, you come to the crushing conclusion that you were never seen as a human being with feelings and thoughts—you were just a vehicle to get closer to what they wanted.

The minute you didn't obey them or do as they asked, you become worth less and less in their eyes. Someone who you thought was vulnerable with you, and who you felt very personal and vulnerable with, turns out to be someone just trying to hurt you for their personal gain.

However, the abuser will very rarely discard their victim of their own volition. They usually want to keep their victim around for as long as possible, squeeze every last bit of "use" out of them as much as they can. When the victim understands that they're being abused, they might try to leave the relationship almost immediately. Unfortunately, the victim—an empathic one, in particular—will still likely have some kind of attachment to their partner. They still feel the need to help them, even if they also want to leave and distance themselves from that emotion. This need to help others, even if they don't really deserve that treatment, is usually what drives the victim back to their partner. If this isn't the case, most abusers also know just how to get their victims back where they want them.

A staple of abusive personalities is that the "best" and most manipulative abusers are incredibly charismatic. They understand precisely how to get to their victims and make them feel loved again. They might suddenly turn up in behavior, begin rewarding them with presents and genuine sentiment again. Most importantly, they'll credit this change to them.

Assuring their victim that they've helped them be a better person reverses the feelings that the victim might have had prior. They go back to the abuser, thinking that things will be different now that the partner has started being better and more in control of their actions.

In reality, however, this is usually just a part of the abuser's plan. They know that they don't have to change, and they never plan to. They just know that they have to do this over and over for as long as they need until they have everything they wanted out of that victim. They'll keep acting out and trapping the victim in the cycle of abuse, then pulling them back in with a feigned change of heart just as they're about to quit on the relationship and leave.

It seems hard to believe that someone would fall for this same trick more than once—it's difficult for most people to give out chances beyond the second mistake. However, victims of abuse are connected to other victims of abuse. They feel compelled to stay with them and to make good on the love and attention that they never got to receive themselves.

In a way, the victim trying to care for their partner is the victim attempting to live vicariously through the people they try to help. The abuser of that victim, who has probably long given up on healing properly from their own experiences and trauma, understands this desire and is sure to take advantage of this at every turn. As time progresses, the victim feels more and more lost. They keep going back and forth between the hope that they can improve their own relationship and the crushing defeat when they go back only to visit that same conclusion—that they're going to be trapped in that relationship with someone who mistreats them.

This is the entire over-arching dilemma of an abusive relationship. When the abuser grows tired of the false kindness, they make all bad things feel as though they're the fault of the victim. The victim is used to having these feelings pushed on them, and they rarely learn how to really deal with that blame coming from other people, in addition to coming from their own internal narrative. They don't want to feel as though they're the root of all their relationship problems, but they also can't help but instill this own fear inside them.

Once you can get rid of this crushing fear inside you and shed the responsibility you feel over the wellbeing of other people, especially other people in your life who might not even care about you, you can learn to actively defend yourself against your abuser's emotional manipulation tactics. You can unlock the part of your life that you were meant to live—the part which is full of love and care, the part that was always waiting for you. This part of your life may have been held back from you by other people trying to pull you down, but you're the only one who can truly unlock it for yourself.

Chapter 10 Using mindfulness to manage emotions

Overcoming narcissistic abuse is one of the most difficult things you might ever experience. It takes a lot of effort to find the momentum to jump from the pain that has engulfed your life to a better future. The most natural reaction to abuse is pain. Your life is shattered, your heart is broken, you lose everything. But all is not lost. There are solutions for you, effective solutions that will help you get your life back.

Meditation

Narcissistic abuse leaves victims in emotional trauma. The kind of trauma you experience in such a relationship has long-lasting effects on your life. One of the most effective ways of healing, managing and overcoming the negativity you experience from a narcissist is meditation.

Meditation is useful for virtually any condition that is either caused or exacerbated by stress. Meditation helps your body relax, in the process reducing your metabolism rate, improving your heart rate, and reducing your blood pressure (Huntington, 2015). It also helps your brain waves function properly, and helps you breathe better. As you learn how to relax through meditation, the tension in your muscles oozes out of your body from your muscles where tension resides.

The best thing about meditation is that you can perform it even when you have a very busy schedule. You only need a few minutes daily, and you will be on your way to recovery. During meditation, try and focus on your breathing. Listen to the air flowing in and out of your body. This action helps you focus by following the path the air takes in and out of your body. It is one of the easiest ways to calm down.

As the air moves in and out of your body, try and scan your body to identify the areas where tension is high. Observe your thoughts so you are aware of what you are trying to overcome through meditation. It is okay to feel the overwhelming sensations, but do not judge yourself. Recovery is not a sprint. It might take you a few sessions, but your commitment will see you through.

Do not reject your emotions. Your emotions are a part of who you are. It is normal to react in a certain way to someone's actions or behavior towards you. Embrace the feelings and overcome the negativity. Meditation will help you make the neural pathways to and from your brain healthier and stronger by increasing density of grey matter. You learn to be mindful of your feelings and emotions again, and with time, you break the toxic connection you had with your narcissistic abuser.

Trauma and distress affects your brain by disrupting parts of the brain that regulate planning, memory, learning, focus, and emotional regulation. Over the years, meditation has proven a useful technique in overcoming these challenges by improving the function of the hippocampus, amygdala and prefrontal cortex.

As a victim of narcissistic abuse, once your abuser gets control over your life, you have nothing else but to follow their command. However, meditation gets you back in control of your life. You can reclaim your realities, heal and become empowered to overcome all challenges you experienced under their control.

Group therapy

Group therapy is one of the options you can consider when healing from narcissistic abuse. One of the first things you will learn in group therapy is that you cannot fix your narcissistic abuser. However, what you will learn is how to deal with narcissism.

Most of the time victims are encouraged to walk out of such abusive relationships, because there can only be hurt and trauma from them. Narcissists are ruthless in their pursuit of adulation, attention and gratification. They are aware that what they seek is impossible to achieve, so they delude themselves in the idea that they can make you achieve it for them.

Group therapy for narcissistic abuse is helpful because you get one thing you haven't had in a very long time, support. Each time you hear about the experiences of other group members, you realize you are not alone. The overwhelming feelings you have been going through become lighter, because you learn that there are people out there who can relate to what has been eating you inside.

While group therapy has its benefits, you will have to play your part to enjoy these benefits. Your willingness to heal is signified by the fact that you are taking the first step to seek help. Commit to the therapy sessions by taking a pledge of what you want out of it. Once you are in, participate. It might not be easy at first because you have to open up to strangers, but you will get the hang of it. It is okay to sit and listen to others tell their story at first. Once you feel comfortable, you can open up. Remember that it gets easier over time as you keep sharing. Never hold back. Therapy is a safe place. By sharing your experience, you are not just letting the group in on your pain, you might also be helping someone else in the group open up about theirs.

Cognitive behavioral therapy

Cognitive behavioral therapy (CBT) is a therapeutic process that combines cognitive therapy and behavioral therapy to help patients overcome traumatic events that have wielded control away from them. Cognitive therapy focuses on the influence your thoughts and beliefs have in your life, while behavioral therapy is about identifying and changing unhealthy behavioral patterns (Triscari et al, 2015)

CBT is effective because your therapist doesn't just sit down and listen, they also act as your coach. It is a healthy exchange where you learn useful strategies that can help you manage your life better. You learn to recognize your emotional responses, behavior and perceptions.

CBT is ideal for victims of narcissistic abuse because it helps them understand their emotional experiences, identify behavioral patterns, especially problematic tendencies, and learn how to stay in control over some of the most difficult situations in their lives.

Cognitive processing therapy

CPT is a subset of CBT. It is one of the most recommended methods of treating trauma patients. Victims of narcissistic abuse usually go through a lot of trauma, and they can develop PTSD. When you develop PTSD, you might have a different concept of the environment around you, your life and people you interact with. PTSD affects your perception of life in the following areas:

- Safety

After experiencing abuse, you are conditioned to feel unsafe about yourself and everyone else around you. PTSD can exacerbate these fears about safety. You are afraid you cannot take care of yourself, or anyone else.

- Trust

Narcissists break you down to the ground. They make sure you can no longer trust anyone, or yourself. In the aftermath, PTSD can cause you to not trust yourself to make the right call.

- Control

You don't just lose control over your life, you depend on your abuser to guide you through your life. Narcissism does this to you. Narcissists are happy when they have control over your life because it shows them they have your attention and can do anything they please with you. After leaving a narcissist, PTSD can reinforce a feeling of a loss of control, which makes getting back on your feet a very slow process.

- Esteem

One of the painful things about surviving a narcissist is the way they erode your confidence. Even some of the most confident people who have ever lived ended up unable to recognize who they are or what their lives are about anymore. You shy away from situations that require confidence and astute decision making, which you would have embraced willingly earlier on. Your perception of yourself is a broken, unworthy person.

- Intimacy

Among other manipulative tricks narcissists use, triangulation makes you feel so insecure about yourself and intimacy. You feel insecure because no one understands you, and at the same time, you cannot understand why they behave towards you the way they do. Following narcissistic abuse, PTSD may give you moments of flashbacks to the points when your intimacy was insecure. It can make it difficult to start new relationships.

All these thoughts end up in negative emotions clouding your life, like anger, guilt, anxiety, depression, and fear. Through CPT, you learn useful skills that help in challenging these emotions. The negative emotions create a false sense of being that embeds in your subconscious, making you feel like a lesser being. CPT helps by repairing your perception of yourself and the world around you. You learn how to challenge the abuse and gain a better, positive and healthy perspective of your life.

Yoga

For a trauma survivor, yoga can offer an avenue to healing. The restorative benefits of yoga have long been practiced in Eastern traditional societies for wellness. Yoga helps you establish a connection between the mind and your body. It helps you stay grounded. This is one of the things that you need when you survive a narcissistic relationship.

Yoga has been demonstrated in the past to be effective in treating different physical and mental conditions, trauma-related problems, and stress (Criswell, Wheeler, & Partlow Lauttamus, 2014). By combining breathing exercises, physical movement and relaxation, yoga helps you cultivate mindfulness and become more aware of your environment, internal and external.

Breaking up and walking out of a relationship with a narcissist is just the first step. Healing takes more steps. You need to find your bearings. You need to end the confusion that has engulfed your life to the point where you lack an identity.

During yoga, you will focus on breathing exercises. Breathing is one of the most effective and free ways of getting relief. Whether you are going through a difficult period, emotional upheaval or a moment of anxiety, all you have to do is breathe.

Each time you feel the urge to bring the narcissist back into your life, find a comfortable place where you can sit quietly and relax. Close your eyes and breathe. Focus on your breathing, counting your breaths to take your mind away from the problem. Gentle yoga classes can help with this.

Art therapy

Art therapy is founded in the idea that mental well-being and healing can be fostered through creativity. Art is not just a skill, it is also a technique that can be used to help in mental health. Art therapy has been used in psychotherapy for years. Art allows patients to express themselves without necessarily talking to someone about what they feel.

It is ideal for people who struggle to express themselves verbally. Art can help you learn how to communicate better with people, manage stress and even learn more about your personality. Through art therapy, experts believe that their patients can learn how to solve problems, resolve conflicts, ease stress, learn good behavior, develop or sharpen interpersonal skills, and increase their esteem and awareness (Lusebrink, n.d.)

Art therapists have a lot of tools at their disposal that can be used to help you overcome the trauma of a narcissistic relationship. From collages, to sculpture and painting, there is so much to work with. Art therapy is recommended for people who have survived emotional trauma, depression, anxiety, domestic abuse, physical violence and other psychological problems from an abusive relationship with a narcissist.

The difference between an art therapy session and an art class is that in therapy, the emphasis is on your experiences. Your imagination, feelings, and ideas matter. These are things that your narcissist partner might have conditioned you to give up. You will learn some amazing art skills and techniques, but before you do that, your therapist will encourage you to express yourself from deep within. Instead of focusing on what you can see physically, you learn to create things that you imagine or feel.

EMDR

Eye Movement Desensitization and Reprocessing (EMDR) is another technique that you can consider to heal from narcissistic abuse. It is a technique that helps to reprogram your brain away from trauma, so it can learn how to reprocess memories. Exposure to persistent trauma might see your brain form a pattern which perpetuates the negativity you have experienced for a long time (Mosquera & Knipe, 2015)

Traumatic memories cause victims a lot of psychological distress. EMDR is a unique method of treatment because you don't have to talk through your feelings and problems. The brain is instead stimulated to change the emotions you feel, months or even years after you walk away from a narcissist.

EMDR works because the eye movement enables the brain to open up, making it easier to access your memories in a manner that the brain can reprocess in a safe environment other than the environment in which your trauma was perpetuated. After accessing your memories, it is possible to replace them with more empowering feelings and thoughts, so that over time you dissociate from the pain and embrace more fulfilling responses to the triggers in your environment. Flashbacks, nightmares, and anxiety soon become distant memories as you embrace a new life and free yourself from their hold.

For victims of narcissistic abuse, your brain remembers the painful memories of verbal, sexual, psychological, emotional and even physical abuse. In an EMDR session, you are encouraged to focus on the details of any such traumatic events, while at the same time viewing something else for a short time.

What happens is that while you focus on both the negative memories and a new positive affirmation, your memory feels different. You will also learn self-soothing techniques to help you continue dissociating from the pain. EMDR helps to unchain the shackles in your life and allow your brain to think about experiences differently.

Self-hypnosis

Hypnotherapy has been used successfully to help victims of narcissistic abuse heal for so many years. There are specific conditions that must be met however, for this to work. You must ensure you are in the presence of specific stimuli that can encourage hypnosis. You will also learn how to narrow down your focus and awareness, and finally, allow yourself to freely experience your feelings without making a conscious choice to do so.

Narcissists are not capable of genuine connection, but instead they project their feelings and insecurities about loneliness and abandonment to their victim. How do you get into a trance state for hypnosis? Emotional abuse has a significant impact on your life. Hypnosis allows you to relax effortlessly. Effortless relaxation is one of the last things you might have experienced throughout your ordeal with a narcissist. The moment you are capable of allowing yourself to relax without struggling, you open doors to healing your mind and your body.

Self-hypnosis is a transformative process that restores your belief in yourself, encourages you to learn important emotional tools that can help you recover from abuse, and also help to protect yourself in the future. With each session, you become stronger, and calm. The waves of emotional upheaval you used to experience reduce and you become at peace with yourself and your environment.

Self-hypnosis also gives you a clearer picture of what your life is about. You let go of the negative vibes and embrace peace. You are set on a path to rediscovery. You find more value in yourself than you ever had throughout your narcissistic relationship. As you go on with these sessions, you learn how to take the necessary steps towards healing, and moving in the right direction in life. The most important thing behind self-hypnosis is that you start looking forward to a new life, and you actually believe in your ability to succeed while at it.

Aromatherapy

Even though it might feel like you are at the edge of a cliff and there is no way back for you, it is possible to recover from narcissistic abuse. Many people have done it before and you can do it too. Recovery from this kind of trauma is very sweet. Each time you make progress, you can look back at how far gone you were, and the changes you have made. It helps you appreciate your life, and realize how toxic it was earlier on.

Aromatherapy is one of the conscious efforts you take towards healing and recovering from narcissistic abuse. Think about aromatherapy in the same way you think about exercise. If you feel you are unfit, you exercise regularly. You can schedule three or four training sessions weekly to help you stay in shape.

The same applies to aromatherapy. Narcissists leave you so unfit emotionally. You need to get your emotions in shape so that you can live a happy and fulfilling life. To free yourself of emotional distress, you need to stimulate your amygdala. Smell is one of the best ways to stimulate the amygdala. There is a strong connection between your emotions and sense of smell, a connection that has been there since you were a child.

The sense of smell is closely associated with emotional connections, whether positive or negative. This explains why each time you smell your favorite food being prepared, it reminds you of an event during which you enjoyed it. Smell, therefore, helps to induce comfort, and nostalgia. If smells can take you way back, it can also help to remind you of the traumatic events that you suffered through narcissistic abuse.

Essential oils used in aromatherapy can help you access emotions buried so deep you never realize they are present (Kirksmith, 2004). They can also bring back memories so that you can embrace them and release those that are no longer useful. The difference between emotions and words is that while they both charge through your body, emotions are faster. It might take you a while to listen, speak and read something during therapy and allow your body enough time to process it. On the other hand, your body will respond to emotions faster. This is why most people are prone to making emotional reactions.

- Basil

- Cedarwood

- Lavender

- Bergamot

- Lemon balm

- Hyssop

- Frankincense

During aromatherapy, you must remember that it is very possible you might not derive the same level of comfort from the essential oils as someone else did. If you don't like the scent of some oil, you might not get positive results from using it.

Chapter 11 The Narcissist's Target

Once you have been able to get away from the narcissist, some of the hard work is going to begin. It is time to figure out the steps that are needed to heal and feel better once the narcissist is out of your life. Healing from the abuse that a narcissist put on you, whether it was mental, physical, or emotional abuse is going to be hard. And sometimes, since you were in that relationship for a long time without realizing what was happening to you in the first place, it may seem impossible even to know where to get started. Some of the different things that you can do to help yourself heal from the narcissistic abuse that you endured includes:

Don't blame yourself that the relationship didn't really work out. If you spent a good deal of your time in a relationship with a narcissist, it is important to not beat yourself up for the challenges that were faced in that relationship. You must remember in this that your partner, no matter how much you loved them, was dealing with a mental disorder, one that you really had no control over. In fact, there is a lot with that relationship that you had no control over at all.

What you can control through all of this mess is who you are in a relationship with, whether you want to maintain this kind of relationship or not, and even your expectations for how the other person in the relationship is supposed to be treating you.

While the narcissist may have tried to take some of that away from you, these are still some of the decisions that you can control.

During this time, there are a few steps that you are able to take in order to help you get through the blame game. First, don't dwell so much on how things have changed, or ever think about how these changes have happened only because of some actions that you took. And, any of the abuse that you received was not your fault, it was because of the narcissistic personality of your partner, and in no way, shape, or form because you actually deserved the abuse.

The net thing that we need to explore is understanding that it is just fine to leave your narcissistic partner. While it is true that most targets are going to fall in love with their partner over the years, it is important to remind yourself that the narcissist does not love you in this process and that this person you thought you loved as changed. Do not feel guilty or allow any blame or shame to come upon you when you are considering whether it is time to leave the relationship and heal from it or not.

Remind yourself during this time that you really do deserve to be with someone who isn't going just to use and abuse you; you deserve to be with someone who loves you and respects you and will show these through actions rather than meaningless words. If you find that you are not getting that out of the relationship that you are in right now, it is time to consider leaving your own partner.

Despite what some may lead you to believe, and despite what the narcissist may have been telling you all this time, it is not selfish to walk out from the relationship and heal yourself. Instead, it is going to be an act of self-preservation that should be done in order to ensure that you get the amount of respect that you deserve.

Once you are out of that relationship, it is time to do your best in order to move on and start a new life. Extracting yourself out of a relationship that is not that healthy can be hard and even emotionally draining at times. Even though this can happen, removing yourself from the relationship that is abusive can end up causing you less pain in the long run.

Getting over someone who you have loved for some time is hard, even if the relationship is bad for you. Remind yourself that the relationship has ended, and it is perfectly fine to feel mad, sad, or a whole bunch of other emotions in the process. This is nothing to feel mad or guilty about at all. Never let this pain and sadness just sit there inside of you. Bottling up the emotions and ignoring them because you don't want to feel bad or you don't want to let the relationship bring you down, is just going to make it worse. If you need to, consider talking about this relationship with another person to help you out.

During this time, you are going to feel pretty sad. You have gone through a relationship that was hurting you for a long time, but it still ended, and this can be hard to deal with. Plus, all of the feelings of insecurity the narcissist sent your way are still going through your head. During this time, remind yourself that you are a wonderful and beautiful person, and you deserve to find someone who truly loves you.

Another thing that you need to focus on here is that you must remember that the narcissist is not really capable of having feelings. It is hard to get over a person who is trying so hard to get you back, which is exactly what the narcissist is going to try to do when they are not abusing you. But to help you not get dragged back into this cycle and stuck with the narcissist again, you have to remember that all of these declarations of love, no matter how much you desire to hear them, are going just to be another form of manipulation from the narcissist to get you back to them.

The narcissist doesn't want you to go. And they will continue to reach back into your life and try to get your healing off track. When you leave, they lose their source of love, their attention, and admiration that they have been getting off you. They will use every technique that they can find in order to convince you back. They will manipulate, yell, scream, talk to you, profess their love and more in order to try and get you back. But they don't mean this. They have not changed, and if you do jump back into the relationship, without actually working on the healing that you need, you are just going to get harmed again.

One thing that you may notice when it comes to healing from a narcissist and realizing that they are incapable of real feelings is that they like to keep their target on the hook. The way that this works is that the narcissist is going to treat the target poorly, but they flip the switch and pretend to be back in love their target just enough times that they can keep the relationship on track and together. In moments where you are reflecting on the relationship, remind yourself of the declarations of love from your partner and see if you can recognize how often these were just another form of manipulation from that person.

During the healing time, it is likely that the narcissist is going to try and get ahold of you. They will call to say that they miss you, that they will change, and that they want to continue the relationship or get back together with you. Try to remember during this time that these words are empty promises and that they are just a way for the narcissist to try and get back in with you. Stay strong, and if you can, cut out all of the communication that you have with this narcissistic person.

You can also work on finding a good support group to help you out. Healing from the narcissist is not something that you are going to be able to do all on your own. It would be nice to escape all of the red tape and emotional drain that the narcissist put you through on your own, but since the narcissist already had you used to the isolation and more, it is time to get away from that and try something new.

Without a good support group behind you to help you succeed and feel better, it is likely that you are not going to see success. This allows the narcissist to have more time to get into your life, to have more chances to tell you that they are the only one who is right for you. They can get into your head so much easier if you let them and without a good support group. Having people around you to keep your spirits up, to remind you why the narcissist was so bad, and to help you figure out the right steps to take now that the narcissist is gone can be so important.

The first person you need to consider getting on your side when you are healing from a narcissist is a therapist. You should work with one who has experience with narcissists and helping targets heal from this abuse. This therapist will be perfect for talking your feelings out with, for understanding what you are going through, for answering your questions, and for being there to give you guidance and the right steps so that you can learn how to let go and live the rest of your life free of the narcissist.

In addition to having a therapist on your side, you may also want to consider having a support group of friends and family members who are happy to be there to support you. If you can contact the people you were close to before the narcissist entered your life, and these people are willing to come back in and be that support that you need, then you are off to a good start.

The trouble here though is that a lot of narcissists made sure that tier targets were isolated. When a target is isolated, they are not able to get the support or any outsideideas that are not supported by the narcissist. Basically, when no one is around to tell the target that they are doing things that don't make sense and no one is there to check the actions of the narcissist, the narcissist is then able to get free reign and has more control.

This may mean that you will come out of this relationship without anyone who will be there to support and love you as you need. This can be a hard realization, but it doesn't mean that you are stuck with no solutions to help you out. You can still find some great people who will be there to support you and love you along the way; you just need to get creative.

Getting out there and making new friends can be a great way to heal from a narcissistic relationship as well. This means that you can't just sit around at home and hope that things get better. You have to get out there, try something new, rediscover your old favorite hobbies or some that are brand new to you if you can't think of any. You have to be willing to jump out of your comfort zone, and perhaps even have some fun. When you are able to do this, then it is easier to have friends and a good support group who will always be there to help you out.

There is nothing better than a good support group when you are dealing with the effects of a narcissist on your life. Many people worry that the narcissist is going to come back and cause problems again. But with a support group who can be there to talk through your emotions with, who may go and meet up with the narcissist with you if you still have to see them, and someone who can help you understand what is normal behavior and what is not when it comes to the narcissist, and it won't be long before you are getting yourself out of that situation, and moving on thanks to your healing.

As you go through this healing process, it is always best if you can try to move on. Extracting yourself out of a relationship that is really unhealthy is going to be hard, and it is often going to drain a lot of energy out of you. Many times, the potential pain is enough to keep people away from even trying to get away in the first place. They have been trained well enough to assume that nothing could be better, and the relationship with the narcissist is the best that they can get, so they never leave.

However, you will find that the pain that you feel inside the relationship, especially over the long term, is going to be so much more than what you are going to experience when you end the relationship. Sure, ending the relationship with someone you truly love, someone who seems like the best person in the world for you, and someone you imagined spending your life with is going to be tough, the emotional, mental, and physical abuse that you went through with the narcissist is going to be so much worse.

It is going to be hard. And there is going to be a time frame when you first leave the relationship where you will question your decisions and wonder if you made a big mistake with what you did. But if you are able to focus on taking care of yourself, and building up a support group, slowly but surely you will start to think about the narcissist less and less. And before on, you will be able to move on to bigger and better things.

Through this part, try to remind yourself often that you are a wonderful person, someone who deserved to be loved by someone, rather than the one who does all of the loving and giving. Love yourself as much as possible by setting aside a part of each day to do "me time" and just focus on something that is good for you something that makes you happy, and something that you love to do. Soon, you will start to see the wonders of this new life without the narcissist, and you will feel so much better.

Take some time to work on yourself during this time. When you were with the narcissist, it is likely that your own self-care was put to the side. You didn't take proper care of yourself at all, because you put the needs of the narcissist ahead of your own needs. Now that the narcissist is out of your life and you are trying to find the most effective ways to heal after all of this, it is time to pay attention to yourself.

Self-care is so important, and it has to be a part of the healing process here. You don't have to go crazy and spend hours a day trying to do this stuff. But even a few minutes a day can make a difference and can help you get back to your old self. The methods you use for self-care are going to depend on your own personal likes and wants, so consider this when making a decision.

Some people decide to just take better care of their health and eat better while working out more. Even half an hour of exercise that you can control can be enough to help with this. Some people go out and purchase the new clothes they have wanted in a long time so they can feel better being dressed up for once. Taking time to enjoy a soaking bath, reading a book, doing meditation, seeing a therapist, and spending time with friends can all be examples of the different options you have available when using self-care for your life.

Eventually, move on and find someone else who makes your heart flutter and who treats you right. In the beginning, it is going to feel like no one else can take the place of the narcissist. Even though they really had no love for you at all, you were in love with them, and perhaps thought that you were going to be with them for the rest of your life. Now that this is over, you are likely going to feel abandoned, and as nothing will ever get better.

The good news is that things will get better. The narcissist is not going to maintain their hold on you forever. In fact, if you are able to remain strong long enough, they will realize that you are not worth their time, and they may go away on their own. And while you should not jump right into the first relationship that presents itself at this time, eventually, you will find someone. You will find someone who loves you and cares about you and who wants to be in the relationship because of who you are, not because of what prestige or other things that you can offer. It may take time, and it is likely to come at a time when you are not expecting it, but no one deserves to be in a relationship with a narcissist, and everyone deserves to find true love. You will find yours when the time is right.

Healing from the narcissist is not always the easiest thing for anyone to do. The narcissist made sure that they were able to have as much control over you as possible. They enjoy being able to get that love and attention, even though they are not sharing any of it back with you. And they understand that if they didn't do the work the right way, then their target would walk away and never come back again.

This is why the narcissist delves in so deeply with their target. They want to make sure that the target stays put and that they are not tempted to run away and not come back again. The healing process, and getting over all of the mind games and more that the narcissist did to you is not always going to be easy. In fact, sometimes it can be very difficult and often the narcissist is going to be able to get back in your head, even with very little communication in the first place.

Taking your time with the healing, and really focusing on yourself can help with this. It allows you to break away from the narcissist, to start to value yourself and to start to understand what is most important to you. Of course, the narcissist is going to be unhappy with the way that things are. They are starting to lose control and are no longer getting their own way. But stick with it, because your mental well-being, as well as your physical health and emotional health, are worth it.

Conclusion

BPD is classified "the Good Prognosis Diagnosis" because, despite the fact that it is one of the more difficult mental health analyzes to contend with, numerous individuals have a high possibility of getting better or recovering altogether. If you have faith in your beloved one and stick by him during treatment, you may see genuine prizes. Many, numerous individuals who once experienced pervasive trouble in interpersonal relationships because of BPD are now healthy and completely functioning after treatment and a ton of self-work. Keeping a receptive outlook, working on your very own portion responses and reactions, and being honest with yourself about the substances of BPD may bring you to a fuller feeling of self and happiness in time.

Living with a borderline personality disorder is hard for the patient and friends and family. If you care about this person, support his or her treatment, figure out how to communicate viably, set limits, and make sure to think about yourself as well. Be patient and understand that BPD treatment sets aside some effort to work. Continue to give appropriate support, and your adored one will show signs of improvement.

The emotional sequence that a person with BPD experiences can be contrasted with a line of dominos. One elicit, one push of the first domino, and the whole range fall in fast succession.

Your responsibility is to attempt to expel your own "domino" from the column. You can likewise realize what makes the dominos fall. Focus on your encounters, and anticipate approaches to keep things quiet. If you can quiet yourself, the adrenaline doesn't course through your structure, and you can begin to attempt to guide the volatile relationship.

www.ingramcontent.com/pod-product-compliance
Lightning Source LLC
Chambersburg PA
CBHW070705250726

48662CB00001B/268